Letters to The Nation

MOLLY IVINS

Letters to The Nation

Edited by RICHARD LINGEMAN

The Nation.

© 2013 The Nation Company, L.P.

Published by The Nation Company, L.P.
Visit our website at www.thenation.com/ebooks

First printing 2013

ISBN 978-1-940489-03-2 paperback
ISBN 978-1-940489-02-5 e-book

Book design by Omar Rubio.
Printed by BookMobile in the United States and
CPi Books Ltd in the United Kingdom.

TABLE OF CONTENTS

INTRODUCTION

RICHARD LINGEMAN

ary Tyler (Molly) Ivins's first contribution to *The Nation* was in 1982. It was a letter cussing out our columnist Christopher Hitchens for some now forgotten attack he had made on a friend of hers, Bernard Rappoport, president of the Life Insurance Company of Waco and financial backer of her cherished *Texas Observer*. Without taking sides in that fracas, I will say that even her mundane letter displayed—aside from a talent for invective—the personal qualities that made her such an esteemed writer at *The Nation* in the ensuing years.

Leading the list was a sense of loyalty to friends and to progressive values. As she liked to say, "You got to dance with them what brung you." Her strong convictions were what brung her into journalism and to us, and most of the time when she wrote she flew her true colors.

By the same token she was fiercely loyal to a lot of friends and colleagues, most of them on the left side of the political fence where she habitually roosted. She had been a founding co-editor of the feisty investigative broadside the *Texas Observer* (joining it in 1970 after working for the Minneapolis *Star-Tribune* and the Houston *Chronicle*). Founded in 1954 by some Texas liberals, a group that could just about fit into the Alamo to make their last stand, the *Observer* was a place, she later fondly recalled, "where you can tell the truth without the bark on it, laugh at anyone who is ridiculous, and go after the bad guys with all the energy you have." For those reasons it served as a farm club and occasional sounding-off board for many writers of national reputation like *The Nation*'s Robert Sherill, William Brammer, Jim Hightower, Larry McMurtry, Larry L. King, Geoffrey Rips, Lou Dubose and others.

Even after she went on to higher if not always better spheres, Molly never forgot where she came from, the small stage where she had found her voice; and she continued loyally to support the paper. Like a lot of independent voices on the left, the *Observer* was chronically broke, so Molly rolled up her sleeves and helped out with energetic fundraising. Reportedly, she raised a total of $400,000 to keep the paper afloat.

And she made a more precious contribution to it and to other left journals—her words. She was a columnist at *The Progressive* and *In These Times*. She once said that she liked to spread her writings around to help out our side. That sounds like ego talking, but she was merely recognizing the fact all those magazines were eager to run her words in their pages.

The Nation was also a beneficiary of her verbal largesse, which explains the contents of this book. Between 1982 and her death in 2007, she contributed eighteen consistently sharp and funny articles to our pages.

One of her friends on the magazine was Hamilton Fish, who was for years its publisher. Ham recalls that when he was still in the process of raising funds to keep the magazine a going concern (which was the *Nation* publisher's number-one job), she shepherded him around the state in the role of a native daughter who spoke the language, introducing him to people who would be useful either as financial or intellectual contributors.

Ham continued to see her through the last years when she was fighting the breast cancer that cut her down too young. Of that two-year ordeal she wrote, "First they mutilate you; then they poison you; then they burn you. I have been on blind dates better than that." Ham says she was always true grit but he sensed how the prospect of death hurt her, a woman with such an appetite for life. Victor Navasky, who had been her editor, saw her during a book tour when he gave a seminar at the *Texas Observer*. She got up from her sick bed to come and hear him and afterward insisted on driving him to the airport.

At her memorial service in Austin the memories flew thick and fast, Ham recalls. A realtor friend of Molly's, a beautiful 55-year-old lesbian, told him she had once taken Molly to see a house. According to Ham, "When she asked her afterwards what she thought of it, Molly explained: 'Honey, I like my houses like I like my men—flashy and structurally flawed.'"

Marcia Ball, an Austin-based R&B pianist, said as she sat down to play at the service: "With Molly's death we've lost a great voice but not a great singing voice." Nobody's perfect, certainly not Molly.

The Rev. Kathleen Jones, who presided over the service, recalled her comment on religion: "Pastors, Molly said, should preach with a Bible in one hand and a newspaper in the other." When she preached from her journalistic pulpit Molly had a newspaper in one hand and a sense of humor in the other.

So how did she first come to write for *The Nation*? The short answer is because the magazine's former editor, Victor Navasky, asked her. Originally, he planned to sign her up as the magazine's television critic, a post we were always trying to fill without success and one that would presumably elicit her wit with minimal demands on her time.

Here is Victor's account of her hiring interview. The next time Molly was in New York, he invited her to dinner at Orso's, an "in" dining spot in the theater district popular with stage folk and first-nighters. Upon her arrival at the restaurant, Victor did a double take. She was dressed in an evening gown and a fur coat. On her 6 foot frame that rig would have looked statuesque to say the least. Maybe this was her way of spoofing the idea of a good ol' gal from Texas trying to make a big impression in the Big City.

After Victor opened the negotiations, she confessed that she didn't own a television set. Victor apparently was not daunted by her lack of experience as a TV critic, indeed as a TV watcher. For she had the one essential qualification for the job: a built-in bullshit detector, fine-tuned on the bloviations of some of the windiest politicians on the Great Plains. And so he offered to buy her one and she signed on.

Time passed, and you know what? She never wrote a damn thing about television.

Instead, she did something better. She started contributing what might be described as Letters From Texas, bringing to the magazine's East and West Coast–concentrated readership the latest political developments in the Great State, which seemed to be full of exotic people known as The Gibber, Governor Goodhair and the left her little to do. Eventually she resigned. "Abe was a hard man to fool," she commented.

A psychiatrist might guess that her double entendre was a subconscious protest. She had been unhappy at the way *Times* editors declawed her prose and dampened her humor. "Naturally, I was miserable—at five times my previous salary," she later said of that period. "The *New York Times* is a great newspaper: it is also No Fun."

Leaving it turned out to be a great career move, for it brought Molly back to the state that was her great subject, and set her to writing columns for the Dallas *Times Herald*, and after that went bust, the Fort Worth *Star-Telegram* and then Creators Syndicate, where she reached 400 papers. Commenting on her triumphant homecoming, her fellow Texan and first editor (later publisher) of the *Texas Observer*, Ronnie Dugger, said that once she got back in her home state she "started laughing…she was suddenly free, free to write funny stuff about politics."

Molly thought covering politics was the most fun you can have out of bed, especially the zany politics of her native state. To paraphrase H.L. Mencken's rhetorical question, Why did Molly cover the Texas Legislature? Answer: Why do people go to circuses.

Nation readers savored her sallies at the Texas "lege," or legislature. Local as her subjects were, they were comical anywhere. She wrote like a ring-tailed-roarer, gouging eyes, kicking ass. "There are two kinds of humor," she told *People* magazine. One is the kind "that makes us chuckle about our foibles and our shared humanity. The other kind holds people up to public contempt and ridicule. That's what I do." That places her squarely in contrast to Will Rogers, the beloved American political humorist to whom she is sometimes compared because he also wrote for newspapers and purveyed a folksy style of humor. But he never met a politician he didn't like and sanded down his jokes so as not to cause abrasions.

Molly's humor was four-alarm Texas chili—spicy, meaty, full of beans. She had a sense of place, and her style connected her with the drab earth of her native land. Writing in a down-home style always poses the risk of being called a phony. Some people, especially from New York, seem to resent folksy humor, preferring the staccato beat of comedy club jokes.

But there was nothing affected about her voice. That was the way she talked, which to my ear sounded just like the way other Texans I knew talked. But even writing in Texlish, she sprinkled her pieces with dudish phrases like "autre temps, autre moeurs," "folie à deux," "sang-froid, "je ne sais quoi." A friend once heard her come out with this amalgam: "The sine qua non, as we say in Amarillo." She was, let's not forget, a third-generation Smith College graduate who had studied at the Institut d'études politiques de Paris and earned a journalism degree at Columbia University. When the occasion demanded, she could write highly literate essays and book reviews like the one republished in this book ("Ezra Pound in East Texas"). She once said: "I have always claimed that being a literate Texan is like being bilingual."

Writing in her native Texlish was her stock in trade, and it planted her squarely in the tradition of vernacular American humor, the big river that runs from Mark Twain to Will Rogers to Ring Lardner...

Whatever language she wrote in, her prose was animated by the mind of an intelligent woman of strong political convictions who believed in honesty, economic justice and equality. With her death, America lost a (non-singing) voice we'll not hear the like of again.

She left her money to the ACLU and the *Observer* but to the rest of us she left her writings, which readers of this essay are now advised to repair to and enjoy and laugh out loud at. Or, if you're reading this online, LOL. ∎

MOLLYISMS: IS TEXAS AMERICA OR VICE VERSA?

"One of the funnier slogans, from George W. Bush's last run for governor, was 'end social promotion.' Social promotion is the story of Bush's life."

"Bush was replaced by his exceedingly Lite Guv Rick Perry, who has really good hair."

"As our former Governor Bill Clements said during an etiquette lesson preceding the visit of Deng Xiaoping of China to Houston, 'We have to be nice to this little fella and remember we all like chop suey.'"

"Many people did not care for Pat Buchanan's speech [at the Republican National Convention]; it probably sounded better in the original German. No one could decide whether Phil Gramm or Pat Robertson made the worst speech of the convention, perhaps because no one listened to them."

"Hearing [George W. Bush] has the charm and suspense of those old adventure-movie serials: Will this man ever fight his way out of this sentence alive?"

"The fact is that unless someone else writes a speech for him, the President of the United States sounds like a borderline moron. But the media sit around pretending that he can actually talk—can convince, inspire and lead us."

"In trying to determine just how far to the right the G.O.P.'s loony wing will go, it's worth noting how Pat Robertson, past and possibly future G.O.P. presidential candidate, is fighting Iowa's proposed equal rights amendment. Pat says feminism 'encourages women to leave their husbands, kill their children, practice witchcraft, destroy capitalism and become lesbians.'"

"The bill to make English the Official State Language came to naught, which is just as well since we'd have had to deport the entire state leadership if it was passed."

"Clements [the governor of Texas]…said he knows the N.C.A.A. has a hard task and he 'commensurates' with 'em and he hopes they 'secede.'"

"Former Congressman Tom Loeffler is now the Reagan Administration's new point man…for lobbying on aid to the *contras*. Loeffler…is the guy who thinks you get AIDS through your feet, as we learned when he wore shower caps on his while on a trip to San Francisco, lest he acquire the disease from the bathroom tile."

"In the line of journalistic duty, I attended the God and Country

Rally featuring Phyllis Schlafly, Pat Robertson and Pat Boone, and am filing a worker's compensation claim against *The Nation*."

"We are also pleased to announce the re-election of Senator Drew Nixon of Carthage: Nixon is the fellow who was found by Dallas police in a car with not one but three prostitutes. He explained he thought they were asking for directions."

"We also elected some railroad commissioners, who more or less—mostly less—regulate the oil bidness, and that makes as much sense as anything else in this Great State."

"I know what kind of governor [George W. Bush] has been— if you expect him to do for the nation what he has for Texas, we need to talk."

"Our only Governor, Sweet William we call him, might be described as irascible. Actually, he's mean, bad-tempered and has a face that would sour milk…. Turns out the man [Gov Bill Vlements] lies like a skunk puts out stink. He couldn't change his mind without looking like a sackful of fishhooks…. Lots of politicians paint themselves into corners by making stupid campaign promises. Bill Clements is one of the few to ever survey the situation and apply a second coat."

"You ever watch a bunch of politicians try to raise taxes and cut services drastically at the same time? Looked sort of like a fire-ant hill what's just been hit with a dose of 2,4,5-T."

"Jim Collins is the man who once moved me, in the days when I wrote for the *Dallas Times Herald*, to observe, 'If his IQ slips any lower, we'll have to water him twice a day.'" ■

LETTER TO THE EDITOR (1982)

What a cheap, ugly shot that was at Bernard Rapoport in Christopher Hitchens's article, "Fashion Parade in Philadelphia" [*The Nation*, July 10-17]. For your information, Rapoport has been on the progressive side of every important fight in Texas for over forty years. Since the Homer Rainey battle in the 1940s, and through the McCarthy era, Bernard Rapoport has been a man the small progressive community in this state could count on, raising money for our great populist Senator, Ralph Yarborough, and for every other progressive candidate who's come along. *The Texas Observer*, the finest regional publication in the country, owes its continued existence to many good friends, and *one* of the best of them is Rapoport. The "old poseur," as Christopher Hitchens so gratuitously called him, has not only been an invaluable public citizen but has performed innumerable acts of private charity, sometimes going to extraordinary lengths so that the recipient does not even know he has a benefactor. I doubt Hitchens would understand the delicacy of feeling that motivates such actions. I am sorry Hitchens did not care for Rapoport's expansive style: myself, I never cared much for snotty Brits. Tell Hitchens to keep his ass out of Texas because there's a bunch of us down here who'd like to kick it from Waco to Luzbuddy.

Molly Ivins, co-editor The Texas Observer, *1970-76*

P.S. Renew my subscription anyway: even *The Nation* is entitled to one lemon on its staff. ∎

H. Ross Went Seven Bubbles Off Plumb (and Other Tales) (1984)

Well, our Attorney General is under indictment. He ran as "the people's lawyer"; now we call him "the people's felon." But it's just a commercial bribery charge; he should get shed of it. We all know there's nothing wrong with Jim Mattox but rotten personality. Meantime, over in the Legislature, the latest incumbent indicted was Senator Carl Parker of Port Arthur, brought up two weeks ago on charges of pushing pornography, running prostitutes and perjury. We feel this is the best indictment of a sitting legislator since last year, when Representative Bubba London of Bonham got sent up for cattle rustling. It's rare to find a good case of cattle rustling in the Lege anymore, so we're real proud of London. Happily, Senator Parker is unopposed, so we expect this to be the finest case of reelection-despite-trying-circumstances since 1982, when Senator John Wilson of LaGrange was re-elected though seriously dead.

Several distinguished former members have been indicted of late, on charges ranging from misappropriation of funds to child abuse. We're running about normal on that front.

On matters cultural, when the World's Fair in New Orleans had Texas Week recently, they invited two of our biggest stars, Willie Nelson and Ralph the Diving Pig from San Marcos. Willie has been galaxy-famous for years now, but this was Ralph's first shot at international exposure, so we were all real thrilled for him. Ralph's the Greg Louganis of porkerdom.

We're having another bingo crackdown: we are big on busting grannies for bingo. If you bingo bad enough in this state, they'll put you in the Texas Department of Corrections, the Lone Star Gulag. Texas and California are running about even to see which state can put the most human beings in Stripe City. We got a three-strikes law here—three felonies and it's life—so we got guys doing terminal stretches for passing two bad checks and aggravated mopery.

T.D.C. is so overcrowded they were like berserk rats in there in the vicious summer heat. There have been more than 270 stabbings in T.D.C. this year. Judge William Wayne Justice, who, in my opinion, is a great American hero and, in everybody's opinion, is the most hated man in Texas, has declared the conditions in the system unconstitutional. Judge Justice continues to labor under the illusion that the U.S. Constitution applies in Texas. Just last year he de-segged a public housing project in Clarksville—almost twenty years after the Civil Rights Act—so the citizens started threatening to kill him again. Anyway, the prisons are being worked on; the Legislature passed some reforms because they knew if they didn't, Judge Justice would. He already made them clean up the whole juvenile corrections system. So now it's just a question of whether the reforms can beat the riot in under the wire.

We have also had educational reform, and it come a gullywasher. First off, our new Governor, Mark White, shows signs of intelligence above vegetable level, which means he will never make the list of truly great governors, such as Dolph Briscoe, the living Pet Rock. So Marko Blanco (all our politicians are trying to be bilingual these days, but as Agriculture Commissioner Jim Hightower says, it just makes most of them bi-ignorant) appointed H. Ross Perot to head up this committee to figure out what's wrong with the public schools. H. Ross took off like an unguided missile. I keep having to explain to foreigners that some loopy right-wing Dallas billionaires are a lot better than others, and H. Ross happens to be one of our better right-wing billionaires. This is assuming you don't make him so mad that he goes out and buys an army and invades your country with it. But he mostly does that to no-account countries full of tacky ragheads, so no one minds. Anyway, H. Ross decided everything was wrong with the schools— teachers, courses, books. The Board of Education had ruled that no one could teach evolution as fact in Texas schools, and H. Ross said it was making us look dumber than the Luzbuddy debate team. Actually, he said "laughingstock." Then H. Ross went seven bubbles off plumb, crazy as a peach-orchard boar, and announced the trouble with the schools is TOO MUCH FOOTBALL. That's when we all realized H. Ross Perot is secretly an agent of the Kremlin; yes, a Commie, out to destroy the foundation of the entire Texian way of life.

The Legislature had a fit of creeping socialism and passed nearly every one of H. Ross's reforms, so now a kid can't play football unless he's passing *all* his courses, and he has to take stuff like math and English. Probably means the end of the world is close at hand. The Legislature even raised some taxes to pay for all this school stuff; first time they've raised taxes in thirteen years, so you see how serious it is.

Economically speaking, Texas is a very big state (it's real embarrassing to have to say that, but they make us learn it in school here). Most economists break it into six zones to report on what's going on. It's not unusual for Texas to be declared a disaster area for drought and flood simultaneously, and our economy is like that too. In the Metroplex, which was called Dallas/Fort Worth back before chairs became "ergonomically designed seating systems," there is just a flat-out boom. The area has technically achieved full employment, 3.5 percent un-. Its building boom should crap out before long, but its economy is almost recession proof—insurance, banking, merchandising and defense contracts. The Centex Corridor (a.k.a. Austin and San Antone) is also Fat City; lot of high-tech firms coming in, supposed to be the new Silicon Valley. But Austin and San Antone are both mellow ol' towns, never wanted to be like Dallas or Houston. Fair amount of no-growth sentiment there, for Texas. But we reckon it's too late: both towns about ruint; gonna need separate books for the White Pages and Yellow Pages before long. The land sharks are in a greed frenzy, turning over sections every couple months for another $1 million, building all over the aquifer. There never was much around Houston or Dallas to crud up, but the limestone hills and fast rivers of Central Texas—that's a shame.

Contrarywise, the Rio Grande Valley's a disaster area. It's truck-farming country, mainly citrus, and also the most Third World place you can find in the U.S. of A. In fact, it's still feudal in some ways. The Valley was already reeling from the peso devaluation last year—we're talking as high as 50 percent unemployment in some Valley counties—when the big freeze hit right after Christmas and just wiped out the whole crop. Now the question's not how widespread unemployment is; it's how widespread hunger is, how bad malnutrition is. A real mess. The Governor and the churches have been great; the Reagan Administration, zero.

Also hurting real bad is most of West Texas. This drought has cut so deep the ranchers have even had to sell off their starter herds. Just nothing left. The Panhandle, the Plains, even in Central Texas, there's no pasture. A goddamn drought is just the sorriest kind of calamity. A flood, a hurricane or a tornado hits and then it's over, but a drought takes a long, long time to kill your cattle and your spirit, and gives you so many, many chances to get your hopes up again—in vain. You folks back East, your beef's going up considerable; we got nothing to start over with when this does break. Our farmers are bleeding to death. Mark White carried every rural (we pronounce that "rule") area in this state in 1982 against a Republican incumbent with more money than God. But one of the laws of politics is It Ain't a Trend Till You've Seen It Twice. The polls show Reagan winning Texas with 75 percent of the vote.

Politically, we've got more talent in statewide office now than in living memory: not a certified Neanderthal in the bunch, and the Treasurer, Ann Richards, is one of the smartest, funniest people in politics anywhere. Our populist Ag Commish, Jim Hightower, keeps us amused with his observations: "Why would I want to be a middle-of-the-road politician? Ain't nothin' in the middle of the road but yellow stripes and dead armadillos." (Tell the truth, I also had a great fondness for Hightower's predecessor, an entertaining linthead named Reagan V. Brown, who wanted to nuke the fire ants. Brown probably lost because he called Booker T. Washington a nigger, but there were extenuating circumstances: he called him a *great* nigger.)

Our Congressional delegation still boasts enough wood to start a lumberyard. We've got a helluva U.S. Senate race. In one corner is Phil Gramm, the former Boll Weevil Democrat, now a full-fledged Republican, named the most right-wing member of Congress by the *National Journal.* Man makes Ethelred the Unready look like a radical. And in the other corner, a 38-year-old liberal State Senator from Austin named Lloyd Doggett: smart, clean, hard-working Mr. Integrity, actually looks like the young Abe Lincoln. If you could jack up Doggett and run a sense of humor in under him, he'd be about perfect. Ever since I mentioned that in a column, Lloyd's been working real hard on his sense of humor.

Doggett's a long shot because there is an ungodly amount of right-wing money in this state, and no decent newspapers, except for the *Dallas Times Herald.* (I'd say that even if I didn't work for it.) Gramm is running a charming campaign, accusing Doggett of being soft on queers and Commies. That usually sells well down here. Doggett can get pretty nasty his own self, in down-populist fashion. Right now he seems to be concentrating on convincing the corporate types that Gramm's so far gone in ideology he doesn't have enough sense to protect the state's economic interests. We used to have a Congressman like that from Dallas name Jim Collins. The rest of the guys would be trying to sneak gas deregulation past the Yankees, and Collins would go into a diatribe about school busing. He didn't just miss the play; he never understood what *game* it was.

People always try to tell you how much Texas is changing. Hordes of Yankee yuppies have moved in, and we have herpes bars, roller discos and other symptoms of civilization. I think, though, maybe Texas is in a permanent state of *plus ca change*. While it is true that there are Texans who play polo and eat pasta salad, the place is still reactionary, cantankerous and hilarious. ∎

THE GIBBER
WINS ONE (1985)

S ummer's going to end any week now, as South Texas temperatures dwindle slowly out of the 90s, and none too soon, let me add, because it's been a real bastard. You could tell as far back as April it would be brutal: the Legislature ran more than usually amok, passing all manner of anti-Bubba laws. Bubba has to buckle up now and all this other bushwa. Thank God it's still legal to drink while driving.

By May the Lege had screwed things up so bad they had to be called back in special session. The most depressing thing about the Lege these days is that it has Republicans in it. Most of them are meanmouth Republicans, too. Warren Burnett, the distinguished legal counselor from Odessa, always advises you should never let anyone on a jury whose mouth puckers smaller than a chicken's asshole. You look at those statehouse Republicans and near every one is meanmouthed like that, mean-dispositioned too. They had a snit because the Democrats came up with an indigents' health care plan, which means we're not going to let poor folks die in the streets anymore. The Republicans and the mean Democrats almost defeated the bill; it came down to a tie vote in the House and Speaker Gib Lewis, a man we seldom think of as a hero of the people, had to break the tie.

It's possible that the Speaker is smarter than we think he is, but it's hard to tell because he can't speak English. Sometimes you listen to him fighting to express himself—valiantly trying to battle his way out of a sentence while surrounded by dangling modifiers, mismatched predicates and loose clauses—and you have to feel compassion. The Gibber's greatest moment this session came on Disability Day, which we have every year to honor the crippled folks for their efforts to get better access to public buildings. We never give them any money for this, but we honor their efforts to get it. Anyway, the Guv issued a proclamation, both houses just resoluted up a storm and Gib Lewis read all of it without making hardly any mistakes. We were so proud. Then he looked up at all the crippled folks in the gallery and said, "And now, will y'all stand and be recognized?"

After the session, the Gibber thanked all the members for extinguishing themselves and left for South Africa. This had nothing to do with politics. Gibber likes to shoot harmless animals, preferably rare ones, for fun. It's his major passion in life. Some nit-pickers criticized him for letting the South African government pay for the trip, but he came back and said out loud, clear as anything, "Those people over there have a lot of problems," which made everything jake.

In July the twinkles on the State Highway and Public Transportation Commission took leave of their senses and announced a new slogan for our license plates: "Texas: The Wildflower State." Bubba hated it. Fifty-six State Legislators signed a letter of protest against it. Representative Jim Rudd said, "I don't want to be the

Wildflower State and I don't want to be the Gay Rights State either." The commission finally backed down. Bob Lanier, the chair, said, "I got the idea the slogan was probably not adequately macho." All this led to a pleasant summer vogue for thinking up great license plate slogans: "Rhode Island: Land of Obscurity." "Oklahoma: The Recruiting Violations State." "Maine: Home of George Bush."

Texas Democrats are enough trouble. Why the hell anyone ever thought we needed two political parties down here is beyond me. Over in the First Congressional District, much of July was devoted to proving that we don't. Thanks to Senator Phil Gramm, who is always busier than an anthill what just been stepped on, the last Congressman from the First is now on the Federal bench, so we had to elect a new one. The Republicans decided this was a test run for 1986 and sent platoons of consultants, image-makers, fundraisers and assorted experts down to Texarkana—which serves them right. Their headquarters looked like I.B.M., all shiny and telephones with lots of buttons and such. The Democrats were working on card tables again in back rooms where the ceilings were falling down. How come Democrats keep thinking they can win when they're being outspent three to one? It's dumb.

Anyway, the Republicans had a terrific candidate, name of Edd Hargett. (One of those experts discovered that people with double letters in their names are considered more reliable by voters.) Edd Hargett has great hair and he not only played football, he was quarterback for Texas A & M. The Democrat was Jim Chapman, who is seriously bald and otherwise just your average Texas D.A., a guy who has devoted the best years of his life to making sure that perps who stick up liquor stores do life in prison. (Which reminds me, a perp in Lubbock got seventy-five years this summer for stealing sixteen frozen turkeys, which is fairly strong gargle given that all sixteen turkeys were recovered, still frozen. Not only no damage but no defrost and the guy still bought 4.7 years a bird. Don't ever steal a turkey in Lubbock.) The Republicans put up billboards *all* over saying, "Vote for Edd Hargett, a Congressman in the East Texas Tradition." This annoyed the Democrats: never been a Republican elected in East Texas before. So the Chapman people went around putting bumper stickers that said "Republican" on Hargett's billboards. The Hargetts called the Chapmans to complain their billboards were being "defaced." This made the Chapmans very happy.

Chapman is the guy who discovered that trade policy is an issue, which is why you too are now being bored to hives over it. Actually no one in East Texas gives a rat's ass about it either, but Hargett was dumb enough to say he didn't see what trade policy had to do with jobs in East Texas. (This view can be easily explained: he went to A & M when Phil Gramm taught economics there.) When Lone Star Steel shut down its plant two years ago, it threw 4,000 people out of work. When Hargett and Chapman had their big television debate, Chapman brought along a "Vote for Edd Hargett" gimme cap and showed the audience the tag on it—said, "Made in Taiwan." Them Republicans may have a lot of buttons on they phones, but they still asleep at the wheel. Chapman won with 51 percent.

August brought a wondrous event, a peace demonstration in the Panhandle. It's not easy to be for peace in Texas. A while back there was an article in *The New York Times Magazine* about New York intellectuals, which was one of the funniest things I ever read. An intellectual named Norman Podhoretz was quoted complaining about the "dominant liberal culture." To prove that liberal culture is indeed dominant, Podhoretz inquired indignantly, "Have you ever met *anyone* who was against a nuclear freeze?" Lord, I haven't laughed that hard since the Governor held a press conference to announce he wasn't crazy. I love New Yorkers, they're so provincial. Bubba's pickup has a bumper sticker that says, "Freeze Now, Fry Later."

Anyway, all the pinko peace lovers of Texas—that's about seventy people out of 16.4 million and most of 'em from decadent places like Houston and Dallas—went up to Borger on the occasion of the fortieth anniversary of the bombing of Hiroshima. Borger is near Amarillo and Amarillo is near what looks like a girdle factory but is actually the place where nuclear warheads are manufactured. So here's a bunch of peace lovers camped in a ditch outside a nuke factory in the middle of August in the middle of the Panhandle. And the good people of Carson County already figured peace lovers were crazy.

The chief thing about peace people is that they're earnest. For three days they prayed a lot, sang folk songs and held seminars on nonviolence in order to prevent nuclear war. Local fundamentalists came by in a truck with a bullhorn every day to tell the peace lovers that peace does not come through disarmament; it only comes when you let Jesus into your heart. One peace lover, Dr. Larry Egbert of Dallas, thought it would be nice for all the peace folk to give blood to the local blood bank. Blood banks're always desperate for donors and this would show that the peace folk are just against nukes, not against the people who make their livings building the bombs. Well, it would have been a cordial gesture, but the Amarillo blood bank rejected their blood. The director told Egbert, "We don't want to get involved in politics." (He later took blood from those who came into town but still refused to send out a bloodmobile.)

At the end of the camp-out, the most hard-core non violents of them all—a menacing horde of nine vegetarians, Unitarians and Quakers—went to sit on the railroad track to stop the "white train" from coming out the nuke factory. That was Against the Law. Trespass, in fact. There's not that much excitement in law enforcement work around Borger, so we had the entire Carson County Sheriff's Department, Borger City Police Department, Highway Patrol and Santa Fe Railroad security guards gathered there to see that the Quakers didn't commit mayhem. We all standin' around in the blazin' hot sun in the middle of your typical Panhandle scene—flat as a griddle, not a tree for 600 miles and everything is one color: dry. Suddenly from out the nuke factory come two black four-wheel-drive vehicles, racing across the prairie, bouncing into the air, whip antennas a-lashin' behind 'em; it is the nuke plant security force. They screech to a halt by the tracks and all hop out. They are wearing jungle camouflage. They are ready to Rambo, lookin' to kill communist revolutionary terrorists. But there's only nine Quakers sittin' on the railroad tracks and none of them has seen *Rambo*. They all went to *Gandhi* instead. That's the trouble with this country, people keep messin' up each other's movies.

What else is new?

§ It's illegal to be gay in Texas again, thanks to the Fifth Circuit. They reinstated our sodomy statute, so people can legally screw pigs in public but not each other in private.

§ Mad Eddie Chiles, one of our better loopy oil zillionaires, is mad again and has taken to the airwaves to tell us about it. All he wants is for the government to LEAVE HIM ALONE, he does not want anything from gummint, except the depletion allowance and the write-off for intangible drilling costs.

§ We're having a football scandal that's so rank it might slop over into politics, which is real embarrassing.

§ Waco, the Vatican City of the Baptists, has hired a P.R. firm for a quarter of a million bucks to "give Waco a more glamorous image." More?

The *dernier cri* for rich Texans is giving money to the *contras* so they can overthrow the Sandinista government of Nicaragua. And it's tax deductible, too. Ms. St. John Garwood of Austin gave $50,000 to buy a chopper for the *contras*, but they're only going to use it for humanitarian stuff, like on *M*A*S*H*, says Ms. Garwood. Buy your own little battalion of freedom fighters; it's a lot kickier than the Cattle Barons' Ball. Why give money to cure cancer when you can kill Commies with it instead? Maj. Gen. John Singlaub, retired, who now heads the U.S. Council for World Freedom, the outfit that channels money to the *contras*, says he gets about half his gelt from Texas. Bunkie Hunt was at the general's last do in Dallas. It's a bizarre concept: the Pentagon, a United Way Agency. What can I tell you? We just have a lot of tacky billionaires. ∎

TOUGH AS BOB WAR AND
OTHER STUFF (1986)

We've just survived another political season largely unscathed. I voted for Bobby Locke for governor: he's the one who challenged Col. Muammar el-Qaddafi to hand-to-hand combat. In the Gulf of us. On the Line of Death. At high noon. Next Fourth of July. "Only one of will come out of the water alive," said Locke. Locke thinks the trouble with America is that we've lost respect for our leaders and this would be a good way to restore same. Me too. Besides, you should have seen the other guys.

The Republicans had a Congressman running who thinks you get AIDS through your feet. That's Representative Tom Loeffler of Hunt, who is smarter than a box of rocks. His television advertisements proudly claimed, "He's tough as bob war" (bob war is what you make fences with), and also that in his youth Loeffler played football with two broken wrists. This caused uncharitable persons to question the man's good sense, so he explained he didn't know his wrists were broken at the time. Loeffler went to San Francisco during the campaign to make a speech. While there, he wore shower caps on his feet while showering lest he get AIDS from the tile in the tub. He later denied that he had spent the entire trip in his hotel room. He said: "I did walk around the hotel. I did see people who do have abnormal tendencies. I'd just as soon not be associated with abnormal people." If that's true, what was he doing running for governor of Texas?

Perhaps Loeffler's most enduring contribution to Texas political lore was a thought that seemed to him so profound he took to repeating it at every campaign stop and during televised debates as well: "As I have traveled around this state, many people have said to me, 'Texas will never be Texas again.' But I say they are wrong. I say Texas will *always* be Texas." Hard to add anything to that.

On the Democratic side, the nerd issue was dominant. The ugly specter of nerditude was raised by A. Don Crowder, a candidate from Dallas. Crowder's platform consisted of vowing to repeal the no-pass, no-play rule on account of it has seriously damaged high school football and is un-American, un-Texan and probably communist inspired. No pass, no play was part of the education reform package enacted last year by Governor Mark White and the State Legislature. If you don't pass all your school subjects, you can't participate in any extracurricular activities, including football. Quite naturally this has caused considerable resentment and could cost White the governorship. So A. Don Crowder holds this press conference in which he says the reason Mark White favors no pass, no play is because White was "one of the first nerds in Texas." As evidence, Crowder produces White's high school annual, and there it was: the guy was zip in extracurricular activities in his school days. We're talking, not even Booster Club. Not Glee Club or

Stage Crew. Not even the Prom Poster Committee. According to Crowder, this explains "the psychological reasoning behind White's dislike of football."

There were headlines all over the state: "Gov. White Called 'Nerd' By Yearbook Wielding Foe." "Nerd Charge Merits Scrutiny." Meanwhile, we tracked down Donnie Crowder's high school annual and guess what? He was captain of the football team. Played baseball. Ran track. And was in the French Club. French Club! Need I say more? *Quel fromage.*

White's initial response to this slanderous aspersion was to whine about how tacky it was for Crowder to be *so* ugly right after the explosion of the shuttle Challenger. Nerd City. Then his campaign manager tries to pull it out by saying, the guy was not real active in high school—but he was super-involved in after-school activities at the Baptist Church. Nerd! Nerd! Finally White gets his act together, comes out and says, Look, grew up poor. His daddy had an accident when the guy was just a sophomore and he couldn't work after that, so the guy spent his high school years working summers and after school. While A. Don Crowder was in French Club, doubtlessly conjugating highly irregular verbs with busty cheerleaders over the paté and vin rouge, our Governor was out mowing lawns, frying burgers and pumping gas to help his dear old silver-haired mother. Great stuff. Besides, Bubba never joined no French Club.

Marko Blanco, as we call him in South Texas, will meet former Governor Bill Clements for a rematch in November. Clements was defeated by White four years ago on account of he's an awful grouch. Grumpy versus the Nerd—what a match-up.

Also contributing to the political festivities of late is that peerless, fearless commie-hater Charlie Wilson of Lufkin. When folks started calling from around the state, and indeed the nation, a month or so back saying, "My God, do you realize there's a Texas Congressman over in Afghanistan, killing Russians? And he's wearing black monogrammed cowboy boots, and he's got a former Miss World with him?"—I, of course, replied, "Must be Charlie Wilson." What else can you say at a time like that?

It's possible to get used to Charlie. He has a certain charm. When I called him to verify some of the more bloodthirsty quotations attributed to him in *The Houston Post's* account of his latest trip to the Afghanistan border, the first thing he said was, "The only thing those cocksuckers understand is hot lead and cold steel." I was especially pleased that he took his lady friend, Annelise Ilschenko, a former Miss World U.S.A., along on the Afghan jaunt. According to *The Post*, she is a "dark-haired and sloe-eyed beauty," and you hardly ever find a good case of sloe-eyed beauty in the newspapers anymore. *The Post* said, "[She] went everywhere with Wilson, not even flinching as she sank her high-heeled white leather boots into the thick brown ooze [of] Darra's main street." No sacrifice is too great when you're fighting for freedom.

Charlie told the *Post* reporter he went over there hoping to "kill Russians, as painfully as possible." Myself, I think it had more to do with an observation he made after he got back: "Hell, they're still lining up to see *Rambo* in Lufkin." Patriotism is always in good smell in East Texas. The night El Presidente started bombing Libya, the deejay at Benny B's, a honky-tonk in Lufkin, made all the patrons stand on their chairs and sing "The Star-Spangled Banner." He said if anybody refused to do it, "We'll know you're a commie faggot." Of course, they do the same thing at Benny B's for David Allan Coe's song "You Never Even Called Me By My Name." Sometimes living in East Texas can be a real challenge.

Living anywhere in Texas is getting to be a challenge as the price of oil slides gracefully toward single digits. Texas-bashing seems to be a popular new national pastime. "Let 'Em Rot in the Sun" said a cordial headline in *The New Republic*. Some Northern papers ran stories on our oil woes with heads the likes of "Sorry About That, J.R." I don't see that we've got any cause to whine about this vein of snottiness: some of the Bubbas did put bumper stickers on their pickups a few years back that said, "Let the Yankee Bastards Freeze in the Dark." Somehow I forebode that Yankees going and doing likewise is not going to teach Bubba any manners. The rest of us down here been having poor luck at it for a long time.

I would point out, though, that Texas is not a rich state, never has been. Never even made it up to the national average in per capita income until the tail end of the oil boom, and then we slid right down again. Poverty level here is always among the nation's highest and, according to a recent study by a team from Harvard University, Texas has more counties beset by hunger and malnutrition than any other state. Our second-biggest industry after oil is agriculture, and you've maybe read something about how it's going for farmers these days. Citrus crop in the Rio Grande Valley was wiped out by a freeze three years ago. Now they got drought and 40 percent unemployment, and the peso is still going down: Our banks had their money in oil, agriculture and Mexico. We're losing a lot of banks.

There is no social support system for the poor in Texas. Adults get nothing; children get $57.50 a month. Bubba's got a beer gut he can let shrink some and not be hurting, but almost half the children in this state are black or brown and they have no cushion. If Eddie Chiles goes broke, it's Don't Cry for Me Texarkana; John Connally and Ben Barnes on hard times, search me for sympathy; and I could give a shit about J.R. But that's not who's hurting.

Good thing we've still got politics in Texas—finest form of free entertainment ever invented. ■

PRACTICING NUANCE
DOWN AT LUBY'S (1986)

Texans will be voting with their feet on November 4, in what is predicted to be the most poorly attended gubernatorial election on record. None of the Above is the candidate of choice for the great majority of Texans, and who can blame them? The incumbent adds new dimensions to the concept of "unimpressive," and the challenger is the guy we threw out last time we had a chance.

Governor Mark White is in deep sludge, the economy has gone to hell and the state faces a massive budget deficit. While no one except Bill Clements, the once and future governor, blames this on White, the man's peerless imitation of a weather vane has helped spread the impression that he can't go to the bathroom without consulting the polls. According to *The Almanac of American Politics* for 1986, "Mark White is a man with no clear philosophy." I'd say so myself. It's hard to look up to a fellow who always has his ear to the ground. Still, White is guilty mainly of bad luck—he was governor when the price of oil went from \$32 a barrel to \$9. His chief claim to fame is education reform, a tremendous effort from Texas, under which it was finally agreed that football is not the raison d'être of our public school system. But if Ronald Reagan is the Teflon politician, Mark White is Velcro. Part of the reform package was a competency test for teachers, who like to had a wall-eyed fit over it and now refuse to vote for White.

Dollar Bill Clements, 69, is one of those people who was born with a burr up his butt. He lost to White in '82 because people thought he was mean, a well-founded impression. His political philosophy is, "If you don't have an oil well, git one." Clements made several units—which is what we used to call a hundred million dollars back when we had money down here—in the "awl bidness," which he considered made him fit to be governor and so did 50 percent of the Texans who voted in 1978. When the largest oil spill in history—caused by a rig from Clements's company—was headed for the Texas Gulf Coast, Governor Clements advised the citizenry, "Pray for a hurricane." When he disagreed with a Mexican scholar on immigration, Clements said, "He's just another Meskin with an opinion." His advice to the unemployed is that they should quit settin' around suckin' their thumbs.

There is a large collection of these sayings from Chairman Clements, many of which are being reprised in Mark White's campaign advertisements. They generally combine ignorance with arrogance, two of Clements's most salient traits, but the man's bluntness can also be endearing. You will notice this in the unlikely event you should ever agree with him. He was once confronted by a fundamentalist at a Republican convention, who demanded to know if Clements had been born again. "No thanks," said Clements, "once was enough." He is running hard on the utterly loony pledge that he will never raise our taxes: we face a $5 billion deficit on an $11 billion budget that was tighter than a tick to begin with. We could elect Jesus governor and he'd still have to raise our taxes. But you know Texans you can always tell 'em, you just can't tell 'em much.

Clements went through the spring primaries smiling like Dale Carnegie himself. The consultants had told him he had to overcome his "mean problem," so he tried to convince voters that in addition to having a bad hip joint replaced, he'd had a complete personality transplant as well. We thought Bill Clements was running for governor, but all spring we got Mr. Chips. Fortunately, that didn't last long: Clements now goes about nastily accusing White of "practicing nuance."

Among political consultants, when the candidate is a dog the preferred euphemism is, "We don't want to overexpose the candidate." Clements's people are so determined not to overexpose him, they'd like to send him out of state 'til it's over. He sometimes gets to campaign at the Casden's filling station near Wink, and they let him out for an occasional hand shaking at Luby's in Longview. Meanwhile, he's all over the airwaves, blaming the state's fiscal problems on "Mark White's wild overspending."

Clements and White had one debate. Political debates are sort of like stock races—no one really cares who wins, they just want to see the crashes. If there aren't any crashes, everyone votes the event a total bore. Clements managed not to say anything too outrageous, just the normal political lies, and then trotted out his patented pore-boy routine. "I started out just a pore boy . . . " When Clements was governor, *The New York Times* kept describing him as "a brash, self-made veteran of the oilfields." What nuance. Bill Clements grew up in Highland Park, the wealthiest suburb of Dallas; he went to Highland

Park High School and then Southern Methodist University, where he pledged Kappa Alpha. He did work as a roughneck: a lot of college kids still do, or at least they did until last November.

Clements started this race twenty points ahead of White last spring. By mid-September, White had pulled almost even. But the most recent polls show Clements's lead holding, and most of us think he has the edge. In a small-turnout election, almost anything could swing it. Facing the oil crash and four more years of Bill Clements would have been enough to depress Hubert Humphrey. But Clements, although a miserable governor, makes a wonderful target. When told Clements had been studying Spanish, Agriculture Commissioner Jim Hightower was moved to comment, "Oh good. Now he'll be bi-ignorant."

We are having an equally swell time with the lesser races. The Republicans are quite taken with themselves for having nominated an actual Hispanic for statewide office: Roy Barrera Jr., Republican candidate for Attorney General, is the son of one of John Connally's old henchmen and is thus fated to stalk through life known to all as Roy Junior. He accuses the incumbent, Jim Mattox, of having brought "disgrace, fiscal irresponsibility and scandal to the office." But Roy Junior says he's not mudslinging: "It's very appropriate for candidates to bring out the facts." And it is a fact that Attorney General Mattox got himself indicted for commercial bribery while in office—also acquitted.

But Roy Junior is just piddling when it comes to Mattox-bashing. The man you want for that purpose is the Rev. W.N. Otwell, who says that Mattox is ungodly, a tyrant, homosexual, a communist and a wicked man who does not love God.

Of course, the Reverend Otwell calls everyone who doesn't agree with him a communist, homosexual God-hater, so it's not that much of an honor. Actually, Mattox is a full-blooded Southern Baptist. Otwell is mad because the Attorney General is trying to shut down his home for wayward boys. The General is trying to shut it down because it doesn't meet the state's licensing requirements. The reverend claims that's a violation of church and state and also Satan at work. Right now Otwell is on the lam, ducking the law, a fugitive; but he appears at press conferences. Via videotape. Wearing burlap sackcloth. And answers questions on a speakerphone. Just another one of those episodes that add such *je ne sais quoi* to life in the Greatest State. Otwell ankled on out of Fort Worth to avoid a court appearance at which the state was set to close down the home for troubled youth. He said, "God didn't tell me to go to jail," which is probably true, but getting the Lord to sign off on these things is damned complicated.

Perhaps you wonder why the state of Texas is persecuting a dippy preacher. Goes back to the early 1970s, when the state simply failed to enforce its licensing requirements for private schools. This legal lacuna led to the growth of a Dickensian industry; all manner of persons set up "homes" for delinquent youth. Delinquents from other states were regularly consigned to Texas—the reformatories in places like Illinois were overcrowded and their authorities saved money by shipping the little darlings here. An early example of the beauty of privatization. The homes advertised they could reform delinquents. To that end, many innovative *instructional* techniques were brought to bear on the wayward children, such as putting them in cages, dousing them with ice water and making them scrub themselves with wire brushes. In November 1972, a 14-year-old girl at Artesia Hall, a school in Liberty County, was forced to swallow lye and left without medical care for three days. It probably would have reformed her if she hadn't died instead.

This caused some stink, so the state took to inspecting and licensing those schools and homes, over the objections of the fundamentalists, which continue to this day.

The Land Commissioner is in a tight race against a hospital. Garry Mauro, the commissioner, has a Republican opponent named M.D. Anderson, which also happens to be a fine cancer hospital in Houston. The M.D. Anderson on the ballot is a bartender from Seven Points and no kin to the guy who founded the hospital, but such details seldom trouble our Texas voters, a carefree lot. Mauro is running very scared.

An avalanche of apathy is the safest bet for election day. Students of politics from around the country want to know what the Texas election portends, being as the oil patch is in big trouble. Who will we blame for this mess—the Republicans in Washington or the Democrats in Austin? What will it mean? Does a victory for Clements signal continuing realignment in the South? Does it mean Reagan still has coattails? Or will a White win prove that moderate Democrats shall inherit the earth? Do yourselves a favor, friends, and seek no straws in the wind from Texas. If folks down here can bring themselves to vote at all, it'll be by holding their noses and pushing the lever against the candidate they can't stand the most. ■

THE LEGE HAS A
TAXING SESSION (1987)

The State Legislature met for eight months without cease. They made it a felony to disturb bats. Premature release of turkeys is now a Class A misdemeanor. They passed over the frilled dogwinkle to make the lightning whelk the Official State Shell. Failure to emphasize abstinence while teaching sex education is now against the law. But they just couldn't produce a budget. Month after month rolled by. The fiscal year ends August 31 and the state was looking at a $6.5 billion deficit because of the oil crash. There were five hours left in the second special session called and the state was two weeks away from flat broke when they finally vomited it out—the largest tax increase ever passed by a state government, $5.7 billion worth of pure, regressive taxation. You ever watch a bunch of politicians try to raise taxes and cut services drastically at the same time? Looked sort of like a fire-ant hill what's just been hit with a dose of 2,4,5-T.

But the session was not without its charms. In April, Governor

Bill Clements was moved to describe the legislators as "a bunch of thumping prairie chickens." So the Senate offered a resolution to make the prairie chicken the Official State Grouse. Lieut. Gov. Bill Hobby said, "The question is on en-Grousement: All in favor signify by thumping once. Opposed, by thumping twice." The senators thumped. "The single-thumpers have it," announced the Lite Guy. Do they have this much fun in Nebraska?

In late April, the Governor went on a seventeen-city tour of Texas to convince the citizenry we didn't need to raise taxes, despite the budget crunch. He flew around the state on a plane christened the Rubber Chicken, in honor of the time he threw such a fowl at an opponent. A Democratic "truth squad" went after him in hot pursuit aboard a plane named the Prairie Chicken. The press trailed after both on the Chicken Little.

Our only Governor, Sweet William we call him, might be described as irascible. Actually, he's mean, bad-tempered and has a face that would sour milk. He's been riled nonstop since January, when the press put him in the middle of the Southern Methodist University football scandal. In August 1985, when he was chair of the board of trustees at S.M.U., Clements ordered the continuation of illegal payments to football players—after the school had already been suspended for same by the National Collegiate Athletic Association. So the N.C.A.A. gave the school the death penalty: killed its football team completely for three years.

The Governor's sole charm used to be the impression people had that he was a straight shooter, a politician who'd say just what was on his mind whether anyone liked it or not. Turns out the man lies like a skunk puts out stink. When asked why he had lied to the N.C.A.A., he snarled, "Well, there was never a Bible in the room."

He ran on a promise of no new taxes, which everyone but the voters knew was a lot of hooey. He waffled as far as allowing that the $2.9 billion in "temporary" taxes passed under the last Governor would have to be made permanent, and there he stuck. He couldn't change his mind without looking like a sackful of fishhooks. Lots of politicians paint themselves into corners by making stupid campaign promises. Bill Clements is one of the few to ever survey the situation and apply a second coat.

Texas Republicans seem to be caught up in the unlikely fantasy that Austin in 1987 is Washington, D.C., in 1980, and they are playing the role of Ronald Reagan, come to slay the dragons of "tax and tax, spend and spend." Turn out the lights and call the law. One thing the Texas Legislature has always been is cheap. And now we don't have enough money to pay attention.

Every day the Lege debated some Sophie's Choice. Should we cut off the program for sick children or should we kick 9,000 old folks out of the nursing homes? Do away with shelters for battered women or the program to help teenage mothers? We can save the indigent health-care program if we take $35 million out of information services, but that means the Department of Human Services won't have any clerks or computers—we'll have a health care program and no way to enroll people in it. And so on.

The members continued to put on their usual pyrotechnic display of oratorical skill. Representative L.B. Kubiak of Rockdale said during debate on an abortion bill: "You know, in Roman days, the gladiators used to get their men down, their opposition down, and they'd look up to Pharaoh, and they'd look for a signal—give 'em life or give 'em death." You remember Pharaoh, the Roman with his thumb in his ear?

As the House debated a dental-care measure, Representative Fred Agnich of Dallas popped out his false choppers and propped 'em up on the podium at the front mike to remind everyone what subject they were discussing.

The bill to make English the Official State Language came to naught, which is just as well since we'd have had to deport the entire state leadership if it ever passed. Clements, denying that he ever paid football players himself, said, "Absolutely not. That's just repungent to me." He also said he knows the N.C.A.A. has a hard task and he "commensurates" with 'em and he hopes they "secede."

A bill to establish a counseling program for sex offenders in our state prisons caused a testosterone tough-off. Representative Foster Whaley of Pampa won wild applause with a counterproposal to castrate the mothers: he offered to come down and personally demonstrate the correct method to prison officials with his trusty, rusty stock knife. Representative Gerald Geistweidt of Mason suggested we could solve the repeat-offender problem by loosening up handgun controls (of which we have none) "and we'll blow 'em all away."

The usual bleeding hearts were heard from: When the chair of the Human Services Department protested the elimination of programs for the disabled, Representative Mike Toomey of Houston said, "He's just trying to get a bunch of people in wheelchairs stirred up."

It appeared to be a tough session for Bubba because the Lege finally scuttled Bubba's God-given right to drive down the highway drinkin' beer. This was clearly the work of a bunch of Communists from New Jersey. True, the Mothers Against Drunk Driving (MADD) were for it, but the Drunks Against Mad Mothers (DAMM) had them out-lobbied. The new law puts a $200 fine on drinking behind the wheel, but since passengers can still drink legally, Bubba is expected to hand his beer to Bubbette if he sees flashing lights in his rearview. Nor is it illegal for the driver to hold a brew himself, as long as the law doesn't see him actually sippin' on it. "Bubba's *not* going to mind that. Bubba's smart," said one senator. The Spuds McKenzie amendment, which would have permitted Bubba to pass his cold one to his dawg, was narrowly, defeated.

Beyond politics, the S.M.U. football scandal has kept the populace amused. One of the leading characters is a rich Dallas booster named Sherwood Blount, called the Lone Booster because for a long time he was the only one to 'fess up. I suspect him of being a figment of Dan Jenkins's imagination. When the N.C.A.A. finally called Blount to question him about all the money he'd handed out to ballplayers, Blount cussed 'em out, emerged from the meeting and announced that the N.C.A.A. is "a bunch of Communists."

Some improvements were seen in our civic life. For years people have complained because the Texas State Board of Medical Examiners never does anything about incompetent doctors. In January, the board was actually moved to file a complaint against one Dr. Harry M. Ricketts, so egregious was his record of malpractice. The board ordered Dr. Ricketts to show up for a disciplinary hearing. The meeting was canceled after the board learned Dr. Ricketts had been dead for some time.

We continue to soar ahead in the area of criminal justice. In Houston a few months ago, a guy got thirty-five years for heisting a can of Spam. We are all sleeping more soundly at night now that the Spam supply is secure.

I trust you noticed that former Congressman Tom Loeffler of Texas is the Reagan Administration's new point man on Capitol Hill for lobbying on aid to the *contras*. Loeffler, you may recall from an earlier letter [see "Tough as Bob War and Other Stuff," page 21], is the guy who thinks you get AIDS through your feet, as we learned when he wore shower caps on his while on a trip to San Francisco, lest he acquire the disease from the bathroom tile. Good luck, Mr. Loeffler, and don't forget your shower caps when you go in to see Congressmen Studds and Frank. ■

DUMB BANKERS,
MAVERICKS TOO (1989)

C ries of alarm are ringing through Washington city—
"The Texans are coming! The Texans are upon us!"
Journalistic brethren from the Northeast have called
to inquire, "What does it all mean? Is there a Texas
way of governing? Is there a Texas point of view?" You understand
we are talking about a range of political Texans that runs from
Henry B. Gonzalez, the ancient Chicano radical, who at 71 slugged
hell out of some sumbitch who called him a Commie, to that trio of
displaced preppies Jim Baker, Bob Mosbacher and Georgie Bush. If
you insist on a comprehensive comment, a one-size-fits-all: What
it means, folks, is a serious setback for vegetarianism. Where you
find Texans, there shall ye also find meat-eaters. The only cultural
advantage to being Texan is that we never have to apologize for
being carnivorous.

I gather the nation's capital has yet to recover from the last
time it was overrun by a horde of Visigoths from the Great State,

led by the Horrible Head Hun, Lyndon Johnson. Fear not, Eastern effeters, none of these new guys is going to pull up his shirt and show you the scar from his gallbladder operation. But I guarantee we've sent you two citizens who will remind everyone where the word "maverick" comes from. (The first Texas Maverick was a rancher who refused to brand his cattle, so that if you found an unmarked cow in your herd, you knew it was a Maverick.) The two new Congressional committee chairs from Texas—Gonzalez and Jack Brooks—are as far from Bob Forehead as it's possible to get.

Wait till you see Brooks, the new head of the Judiciary Committee, in action. Come to think of it, you already have. He was the only guy on the Iran/ *contra* committees last summer with *any* guts, remember? The one who kept trying to wade into *contra* drug smuggling and all that other stuff the good little boys had promised to stay away from. The thing about Brooks is that he just doesn't care, except about the Ninth Congressional District, where they think he's God. In the Ninth it is widely believed that Brooks personally ordered Hurricane Gilbert to steer clear of Beaumont/Port Arthur—with powers greater than the prayers of Pat Robertson! Brooks does not give a flying fart about what is seemly, proper, politic, not done, or about whose reputation gets hurt, making it look good, or public relations.

As for Henry B, he's been going his own road for so long no one could make him shape up. It's been chic to snicker a bit at Henry B in recent years—he's overweight, he has an accent and bad hair, he talks too much and believes too passionately in things that are not neo. But I notice Washington seldom snickers long at those with power. Some rainy afternoon, you should get someone who was there to tell you about the time in 1957 when Henry B. Gonzalez filibustered against the segregation bills in the Texas Legislature for thirty-six hours and two minutes. The charm of having Henry B as chair of the Banking Committee during the S&L catastrophe and what promises to be a spirited round of re-regulation is that Henry B understands two important things: Bankers all have hearts like caraway seeds, and bankers as a group are dumb. 1 am pleased to report that the phrase "dumb as a Dallas banker" has now made its way into the Texan language.

We are also pleased to announce the advent in Washington of a new Representative from the Panhandle of Texas, the Hon. Bill Sarpalius of Amarillo. "Sarp," as he was known in the Texas Senate, earned a reputation as a fella not exactly bent over double with intellect, no mean achievement in the context of that legislative body. Many laughed when Sarp announced for the Congress—they felt he had already exceeded his level of competence back when he was first elected an officer in the local chapter of Future Farmers of America. But a wonderful thing happened to Sarpalius right at the beginning of his Congressional campaign: One Saturday night last January, as Sarp stepped outside a local honky-tonk, an irate constituent slugged him and broke his jaw. Sarpalius went through the entire primary with his jaw wired shut, unable to speak—a stroke of luck you will be able to appreciate fully when you hear the man talk.

Also on the list of reasons to cheer the outcome of the November plebiscite was the defeat of Mac Sweeney, a coprolitic Representative from the Coastal Bend. Sweeney is sort of like Dan Quayle without the substance. His television commercials kept proclaiming, "In Washington, when you say the name 'Mac Sweeney,' people tell you, 'He works for Texas.'" Actually, if you say "Mac Sweeney" in Washington, people laugh. Always nice to know Texans will not re-elect a terminal numbskull indefinitely.

Charlie Wilson, the East Texas Representative and hero of Afghanistan (recently lionized on *60 Minutes*, which was a refreshing change, since the last time *60 Minutes* paid any attention to Charlie it was on account of that unpleasant business about the cocaine), came up with a scheme to save Speaker Jim Wright from the nasty schemers who hauled him before the House Ethics Committee. Wilson suggests that no one should be allowed to serve on the House Ethics Committee who has not himself been investigated. He claims this would cut down on the hypocrisy and the sanctimony, would produce a committee of people who understand how much lawyers cost and who could recognize chickenshit when they see it. Wilson was himself on the Ethics Commitee until it had to investigate him: He claims he got the seat by observing to Mo Udall, as he studied the list of the members, "Damn, there's not a sonofabitch on here who likes pussy or whiskey. They're not representative of the Democratic Caucus." Udall agreed and put Wilson on.

The State Legislature convenes in January, but we are trying not to think about it. William Clements Jr., our only Governor, gets meaner and more irrational by the day. We are under court order to fix the prisons, the mental hospitals and the schools for the mentally retarded. We also face an increase in enrollment in the public schools, a state work force that hasn't had a raise in years, Federal requirements to improve nursing homes, and more AIDS cases. But the real hitch in the getalong is a lawsuit that could force the state to equalize funding for public schools. In rich suburban districts there are heated towel racks in the high school locker rooms. In poor barrio districts they can't afford chalk or toilet paper. To get this Governor and this Legislature to raise taxes you have to hold a gun and a court order to their heads and be ready to use both. If there is any possible way to do nothin' about all of this, I fearlessly forecast that's what the Lege will do.

We used to be able to count on Mississippi bein' worse than we are; near as we can tell, it's the only thing Mississippi's ever been good for. But last spring those 'Sippians went and elected a fellow called Baby Ray Mabus Governor, and he got there by running around the state saying to every crowd he could find, "I can't promise you we'll be Number One, but I promise you *we'll never be last again.*" The crowds took to chanting along with him, "WE'LL NEVER BE LAST AGAIN." Guess who that's gonna leave Numero Fifty-o? Our A.F.D.C. grant is still $57 a *month*, per child.

Finest new member of the State Senate is Bill Haley, a funeral home director from Center. Last year some friends took Haley to eat at a swanky Austin restaurant. Faced with an absurdly pretentious wine steward, Haley, who is suspected of being more than mildly literate, became a complete naif. The steward finally came around with a tray of after-dinner drinks. "How much is that kind, a glass?" inquired Haley.

"Zat, monsieur, is $6 ze glass," replied the steward.

"Oh my," said Haley in wonder. "And that kind, how much is that a glass?"

"Zat, monsieur, is ze very best we have in ze house. Zat is $25 a glass."

"Twenty-five dollars a glass!" squealed Haley. "Why, you wouldn't want to pee for a month, would you?"

Cultural notes from around the Great State: A citizen fed up with "lawyers running the country" has filed a $1 billion class action lawsuit against the entire legal profession. Daniel Madison of Austin is suing the American Bar Association, the Texas Supreme Court, the University of Texas Law School and the Law School Council for violation of antitrust laws, claiming they conspire to keep power out of the hands of nonlawyers. "If you're rich, you can have all the justice you want, but if you're a working-class citizen, you may get little or none. That's the system in America and I intend to prove it," said Madison.

Proving once more that the legal profession is a disgrace, Texas lawyers passed up a chance to elect Oliver Heard president of the Bar Association. Heard was caught in a nude modeling studio during a police raid in the middle of his campaign for the state bar office. Heard claimed he just went into the place to use the bathroom, but came to electoral grief anyway.

Justice in Dallas was once again enlivened by that thoughtful jurist, Judge Jack Hampton of State District Court. Hampton, a notorious hanging judge, explained in December that he had given a mere thirty years to a young thug who shot two unarmed men in cold blood because the victims were, after all, only "queers." This incident naturally reminds all serious students of country music of the old Lounge Lizards song, "I am goin' back to Dallas to see if there could be anything worse than losing you." ∎

NOTES FROM
ANOTHER COUNTRY (1992)

Nothing like a Republican convention to drive you screaming back into the arms of the Democrats. Especially this convention. The elders of the press corps kept muttering they hadn't seen anything like it since the Goldwater convention in '64. True, the Republicans spent much of their time peddling fear and loathing, but it was more silly than scary, like watching people dressed in bad Halloween werewolf costumes. During the buildup to the convention, the most cockeyed optimists among the Democrats were in hopes the Republicans would tear themselves apart over abortion. No need. The party was dead meat on arrival.

I am a cautious political bettor. It's silly to put money down any closer than six weeks out from Election Day, and one should never underestimate the ability of the Democrats to screw up. But the Republicans have nothing going for them and nothing they can try works. They got a three-point bounce out of their convention.

The in-depth polling shows the great majority of the public didn't care for the gay bashing, didn't care for the feminist bashing, didn't care for the Hillary-bashing and thought the whole exercise was too negative. It was.

The most surprising aspect of the convention was George Bush, and the surprise was—no surprises, not even a mini-idea. His own advisers were pushing the line that his big speech would finally, at long last, answer all the questions—how to get out of the recession, what the domestic agenda should be and what his vision thing actually is. They even promised that after four long years we would learn who the hell he is and what he really believes. We got nothing.

On the economy, one more *time*, he pushed a capital gains tax cut. There is little historical evidence that a cap gains cut stimulates the economy, and recent studies by academic *economists* (as opposed to the political kind) show that half of realized capital gains go straight into consumption. It's the dumbest kind of tax subsidy to conspicuous consumption you can try.

You can argue, as both Paul Tsongas and Bill Clinton do, that a targeted capital gains cut would be beneficial. Bush not only wants the cut with no strings, he's even arguing for a cut on past investments, which is nothing but a windfall for richies.

The confabulation in Houston was not, however, without its charms. I loved Ronald Reagan's speech (apparently he, not Peggy Noonan, actually wrote it)—especially the line about Thomas Jefferson. Until it occurred to me to wonder what would have happened if Jefferson, surely the finest intellect this soil has ever produced, actually did meet Reagan. Imagine the conversation:

"Ignorance is preferable to error; and he is less remote from the truth who believes nothing, than he who believes what is wrong."

"Well. Make my day."

(Such ruminations may be a consequence of the brain damage caused by listening to Republicans bloviate for hours on end. In the line of journalistic duty, I attended the God and Country Rally featuring Phyllis Schlafly, Pat Robertson and Pat Boone, and am filing a worker's compensation claim against *The Nation.*)

Many people did not care for Pat Buchanan's speech; it probably sounded better in the original German.

No one could decide whether Phil Gramm or Pat Robertson made the worst speech of the convention, perhaps because no one listened to them.

In trying to determine just how far to the right the G.O.P.'s loony wing will go, it's worth noting how Pat Robertson, past and possibly future GO.P. presidential candidate, is fighting Iowa's proposed equal rights amendment. Pat says feminism "encourages women to leave their husbands, kill their children, practice witchcraft, destroy capitalism and become lesbians."

Listening to George Bush, toward the end of his speech, read the poetry written by Ray Price with the gestures scripted by speech coach Roger Ailes, I was struck anew by the elaborate charade of emperor's clothing in which the American press is so supinely complicit. Bush has no more sense of poetry than he does of grammar. After the speech there was much division in the pundit corps over whether Bush had just "hit it out of the park" (both sports and war metaphors were much in vogue) or whether we had just heard a load of nasty political drivel without a single redeeming idea. But all hands were solemnly pretending we had just heard George Bush, the nation's most incoherent speaker, stand up and make a fifty-eight-minute political address.

George Bush without a Teleprompter can scarcely produce an intelligible sentence. I've been listening to him since 1966 and must confess to a secret fondness for his verbal dyslexia. Hearing him has the charm and suspense of those old adventure-movie serials: Will this man ever fight his way out of this sentence alive? As he flops from one syntactical Waterloo to the next, ever in the verbless mode, in search of the long-lost predicate, or even a subject, you find yourself struggling with him, rooting for him. What is this man actually trying to say? What could he possibly mean? Hold it, I think I see it!

Imagine, for a mad moment, George Bush in the British Parliament, where the members are not only fluent in English but expected to think on their feet as well. I am told that public policy is often hammered out in the exchange of thought there. How would anyone ever figure out what Bush thinks? This is not a matter of grammar: Anyone who has ever heard some canny country legislator fracture the language while making his point knows clarity is not synonymous with syntax. The fact is that unless someone else writes a speech for him, the President of the United States sounds like a borderline moron. But the media sit around pretending that he can actually talk—can convince, inspire and lead us.

We have long been accustomed to hearing Republicans exploit racial fears, usually by talking about crime. The "family values" issue is a more subtle exploitation of the doubt, confusion and guilt felt by American women, who are receiving so many conflicting messages from this society that no matter what choices we make, or more often, what roles necessity forces on us—work, family or the difficult combination of both—we all feel guilty about what we're doing. It's quite true that full-time homemakers resent the condescension in remarks like Hillary Clinton's "What did you expect me to do, stay home and bake cookies?" But this is a society in which people's worth is judged by how much money they make, and the esteem in which our society holds wives and mothers is reflected in their salaries.

For a political party that has consistently opposed every effort to build a support network for working mothers to then condemn and guilt-trip them is despicable. Natal leave, parental leave, day care— the whole complex of programs that exist in other industrialized nations to help working mothers does not exist here, thanks to the Republican Party. Most women in this country work because they have to. Most are still stuck in the pink-collar ghettos of sales personnel, clerical personnel and waitressing. Clerical workers are in a particular bind as more and more corporations replace them with "temporary workers" in order to avoid having to pay health and retirement benefits.

The gay bashing at the convention would have been offensive even without the AIDS epidemic. Have they no shame, at long last have they no shame? I watched delegates who are the mothers of gay sons sit there and listen without protest. I don't know what it says about their family values.

I'm not even sure why any of this was discussed at the political convention, except that the R's clearly see political gain in it. The Constitution says the purpose of our government is "to form a more perfect union, establish justice, insure domestic tranquility, provide for the common defense, promote the general welfare, and secure the blessings of liberty to ourselves and our posterity." The President is nowhere designated in the Constitution as arbiter of our sexual morals.

Trying to figure out from whence and why came the nastiness at that convention, I found two sources.

There are lots of nice Republicans in this world, perfectly

decent, quite bright people. When Peggy Noonan, Reagan's speechwriter, covered the Democratic convention for *Newsweek*, she wrote: "There was much talk of unity, but what I saw was the pretty homogenized gathering of one of the great parties of an increasingly homogenized country—a country that has been ironed out, no lumps and wrinkles and grass stains, a country in which we are becoming all alike, sophisticated, Gapped, linened and Lancomed." It occurred to me that Noonan not only did not attend the same Democratic convention I did, she does not live in the same country I do.

Turns out she lives in East Hampton, Long Island, which may account for it. Despite having lost her job at the White House a few years ago, she does not seem to have spent any time in the unemployment line. In her country, people aren't worried about their jobs, they aren't caught in hideous health insurance binds, they aren't watching their standard of living slip slowly down, their hopes for a home slip slowly away, their dreams for the future dwindle. It's another country, the country of those who are Doing Well.

The second source of the nastiness is cynical political professionals pushing divisiveness for political reasons, exploiting fear and bigotry because it works. Old dog. Still hunts.

The professionals around Bush seem, like the man himself, not to believe in much of anything except their own entitlement to power. They are not the true believers of the Reagan years, nor even like the angry lower-middle-class Nixonites feeling snubbed by the Eastern Establishment. Too many years, too many limousines. They're out of touch with the country and fighting like piranhas not for ideas or any vision of a better America—they're fighting to keep their limousines. ∎

MY FRIENDS,
THE TIME IS NOT YET (1994)

Dear *Nation* Readers.

Well, it was a swell campaign while it lasted. My brief foray into electoral politics at the behest of this very magazine swept through Texas like a dose of Ex-Lax. *The Nation*'s nifty notion that I would make a dandy candidate for the U.S. Senate was greeted with acclaim by all twelve *Nation* readers in the Great State.

Offers of help poured in. Ed Rollins called to say he had some leftover walking-around money from the New Jersey governor's race. My pal H. Ross offered to lend me some old charts so I could do well in debate. And a Highly Placed Source said he knew of two former Arkansas state troopers who would be just terrific at protecting my privacy, as soon as they fulfill their new book contract.

Governor Ann Richards was all for the idea, but she wanted me to run as a Republican, using the slogan "Molly Ivins Can't Be a Republican, Can She?" But my campaign manager, Dee Simpson, insisted I run as a Democrat with the slogan "Nothin' But Good Times Ahead." He then went around Austin claiming that Jimmy Mattox was just my stalking-horse.

Those of you who recall former State Attorney General Mattox as the pit bull of Texas politics should know that this year we are being treated to the kinder, gentler Jim Mattox. Only one fistfight so far. It's true that I once observed of Mattox, "He's so mean he wouldn't spit in your ear if your brains were on fire." It's not true that the thought of running against him reduced me to quoting Joseph Conrad over and over: "The horror! The horror!"

Representative Mike Andrews, the other Democrat in the race and the one who looks as though he's just been Simonized, says he aspires to the mantle of greatness left by Lloyd Bentsen. Andrews said, "Ivins, you're no Erma Bombeck."

Richard Fisher of Dallas, the Perotista running as a Democrat, just choked on his money. So all in all, my candidacy was looking good until the wily and parsimonious Victor Navasky, he who pays all *Nation* writers in the high two figures, found out the filing fee for the Texas Senate seat is $4 K. It was Navasky who kept saying, "The horror! The horror!"

Then my campaign was dealt a near-mortal blow by the *San Antonio Express*, which editorialized against my getting into the race on the feeble grounds that my talents are better suited to writing a newspaper column. It's not that I minded the opposition of the *Express*, but at that point, one more Texas editorial board had come out against me than had come out against Senator Kay Bailey Hutchison, and she's been indicted and re-indicted.

So I decided the time is Not Yet, but I'm bearing this overwhelming show of support in mind. Further on down the line, I think it would be excellent to mount a serious un-serious campaign for public office, not to mention being a lot of fun. I'm saving all my campaign contributions from this year for that very purpose.

Meanwhile, we're not off to an auspicious start to the new year here in the Great State. First thing that happened was some University of Texas students allegedly stole Texas A&M's mascot, the dog Reveille, before A&M's big game in the Cotton Bowl. The U.T. dognappers sent a note demanding that A&M admit, "we're better than them." The English faculty of U.T. was mortified. "You teach them and you teach them," moaned one prof, "and still they send ungrammatical ransom notes." No one at A&M noticed. The dog was returned in time for the game, which A&M lost to Notre Dame, and then the Aggies drew five years' probation, no bowl games and no television time, for paying their football players. However, we still think of Oklahoma as "the recruiting violations state."

In our other major sport, you may wonder why our junior senator, the Breck Girl, is under indictment. It came about thusly: Senator Hutchison stands accused of having misused state property and state employees to do personal and political work. Which is against the rules. Also, when John Connally's daughter Sharon was working for the B.G. at the State Treasurer's office, Hutchison, a former University of Texas cheerleader, is alleged to have whacked Sharon on the shoulder several times with a ring binder in the course of pitchin' a wall-eyed fit. This is an uncheerleaderly thing to do.

Now, finding a Texas officeholder who has misused, say, a state telephone for political purposes is not a novel situation. More like, common as dirt. Ronnie Earle, who has been the D.A. in the state capital since shortly after the earth's crust cooled, does not normally get excited about, oh, $10,000 or so worth of misuse. He generally calls in the offending pol and demands that he or she repay the money and promise not to do it again. Unfortunately, the Breck Girl is alleged to have denied something in the neighborhood of $100,000 worth of misuse and then, worse, to have gone back to her office and destroyed records that supposedly proved said misuse. Which leads us to the new rule of Texas politics: Don't Lie to Ronnie Earle. It Annoys Him.

Meanwhile, we are all happy for our former Senator Bob Krueger, who finally has a job. Krueger ran a memorably awful campaign against Hutchison last year. At one point, the former professor of Shakespeare at Duke University informed a union audience in Beaumont, "As we all know, Integritas is the Latin word for integrity." He was speaking to a group of folks who really wanted to know where to get some bait and a six-pack to go. But now the Clinton Administration is considering naming Krueger ambassador to Burundi. They reportedly got the idea from the movie *Dave*. We think Krueger's penchant for quoting Shakespeare and Plutarch may be useful in resolving the civil war now under way in Burundi.

Yours in the hope that your state is looking better than mine for this year,

Molly ∎

SHRUBWHACKED (1994)

As far as Texas goes, the story is simple, and it could have been worse. Ann Richards was dragged out of office by the fact that 63 percent of the people in this state disapprove of Bill Clinton, and of that 63 percent, most of them can't stand him.

Richards won by 100,000 votes in 1990: 120,000 new Texans have since registered as Republicans, most of them in the suburbs.

As Bush Brothers go, Shrub—George the Younger—is not bad. He's less mean and less right wing than his brother Jeb and smarter than his brother Neil. Of course he's a know-nothing little pipsqueak compared with Ann Richards, but then, Richards is pretty special.

Both Bush and Richards ran mistake-free campaigns, but the problem was apparent from August on. One East Texas poll showed Richards's approval at 60 percent, even though she trailed Bush by 11 points. Given her personal popularity, a booming economy, lower crime rates and no scandal, the race should have been a walk for Richards. But Bush avoided attacking her personally and stuck to what he wants to do for Texas. Richards ran on her record without saying much about the future.

Because Texas has what political scientists call "the weak-governor system," a common Southern hangover from Recon struction, Texas governors can't actually do much. Richards knows this, Bush doesn't, so he went around blithely promising to do this, that and the other. Sounded good.

There was literally no contest at the top of the ticket between Kay Bailey Hutchison and Richard Fisher. Fisher's wife reportedly told him he could not spend any more of their money (he spent a handsome chunk of it getting the nomination), so he became a noncandidate right after the primary.

The rest of the statewide offices stayed Democratic, all incumbents returned: The stopper was Lieutenant Governor Bob Bullock, a wily old trout who will doubtlessly be running Shrub Bush's life for the next four years. We had the usual down-ballot catastrophes. We put three stealth Christians on the State Board of Education and we've elected an extremely peculiar fellow named Steve Mansfield to the Court of Criminal Appeals. He has, ah, résumé problems.

We lost two Democratic Congressmen, Bill Sarpalius of Amarillo, who deserved to lose, and the redoubtable Jack Brooks of Beaumont, whose loss demonstrates that the National Rifle Association has the brains of a walnut. The gun lobby set out to get Brooks for letting the crime bill get out of his committee with the assault weapons ban in it. Of course Brooks is the guy who single-handedly almost got the assault ban *out* of the bill. One nice thing about gun nuts is that they have no political sense at all. ∎

Ezra Pound in
East Texas (1995)

Review: *The Liars' Club: A Memoir*. By Mary
Karr. Viking. 320 pp. $22.95.

T his book is so good I thought about sending it out for a
backup opinion. After all, if you're going to announce
something as unlikely as news of a genius from the
Golden Triangle, for pity's sake, right away you've
got a credibility problem. It's like finding Beethoven in Hoboken.

The Golden Triangle (the emphasis is on the "ang") of Texas
consists of Beaumont, Port Arthur and Orange, three of the ugliest
towns on earth, growing like a foot fungus right along the Texas-
Louisiana border. Nothing but oil refineries and chemical plants
for miles and miles, all polluting away industriously so the whole
area stinks. Folks there are white, black and Cajun, and all working
class to the bone. Only place in Texas that's unionized. Lots of trailer
trash, coonasses and tackiness.

And out of this unlikely stew comes Mary Karr, a poet, no less. Her memoir of her family and her growing up, particularly the portrait of her parents, is quite simply wonderful. The Liars' Club of the title was a group of her father's friends who gathered at the Legion Hall or the bait shop to play pool and tell stories. Such stories. Fishing, hunting, snakes, murders, the Depression, all the stuff good stories are about. Her daddy was a decent man and a strong one, but a drinking man too, and etched throughout this memoir without ever being directly addressed is what booze does to people's lives.

Her mama was Nervous, which as Karr notes is Texan for anything from fingernail biting to full-blown psychosis. Mama was from West Texas, where at least the air is clean, an artist who had lived in New York, read existentialists and listened to opera. Naturally the woman wound up *un poco loco*. Reading Camus while living in a culture that considers Roy Orbison a great artist is not easy. Mama wore Shalimar—in the Golden Triangle.

There's a parody of Southern writing by I-forget-who that claims it's always about why-Daddy-blew-his-head-off-after-Bubba-raped-Sissy-the-night-the-hogs-ate-Grandma. Much as I deplore sweeping generalizations, I do believe everybody in East Texas is slightly crazy. I have a great deal of evidence to support this thesis. So when Karr's batty Grandma Moore arrives to die of cancer, the ensuing lunacy is described with what I believe is perfectly appropriate sang-froid. This isn't Southern Gothic; it's just great reportage.

The solution to the mystery of Karr's mama's Nervousness is the denouement of the book, but it comes after so much living, it's not much more than a postscript. Just an old agony. I think my favorite character is Mary Karr's sister Lecia, who is only 10 years old during much of this tale, and definitely someone you want on your side in a fight. I know a lot of Texas women like Lecia and Mary Karr, and I believe they survive because they know how to fight. Literally. As Karr's daddy told her, when they're too big to beat, bite. "'Lay the ivory to 'em, Pokey,' was how he put it," Karr writes. "To my knowledge, I never slouched off an ass-kicking, even the ones that made me double up and cry." We're talking tough women.

I have always claimed that being a literate Texan is like being bilingual, and Mary Karr is a perfect example of that bilingualism. She can switch from Yeats to coonass without pause, from down-home similes about dog shit to Ezra Pound. You can't be pretentious and from the Golden Triangle both. While this book is the most personal of tales—hacksaws and cancer, mockingbirds and water moccasins, Jack Daniel's and Agent Orange, locusts and margaritas, crackup and child-rape—it also contains a number of surprising and tart observations about class. Practitioners of political correctness might want to consider the following passage:

> To this day, it's a peculiar trait of Leechfield citizenry that your greatest weakness will get picked at in the crudest local parlance. In fact, the worse an event is for you, the more brutally clear will be the talk about it. In this way, guys down there born with shriveled legs get nicknamed Gimpy, girls with acne Pizzaface.

> My daddy even worked with a guy whose teenaged son had gone berserk with a twelve-gauge shotgun and marched one summer day into the Junior High, where he shot and killed a guidance counselor while the principal (the alleged target, we later heard) hid in the school safe. The men on Daddy's job right away nicknamed this kid the Ambusher. The week the local paper carried a story

about the boy's incarceration and lobotomy in the state hospital at Rusk, the guys at the refinery pitched the kid's daddy a party complete with balloons and noisemakers. I shit you not. Daddy claimed that the card they gave the poor fellow read: "Here's hoping the Ambusher can finally hang up his guns!"

This kind of bold-faced ugliness was common to us. The theory behind it held that *not* mentioning a painful episode in the meanest terms was a way of pretending that the misery of it didn't exist. Ignoring such misery, then, was equal to lying about it. Such a lie was viewed as crueler, even, than the sad truth, because it somehow shunned or excluded the person in pain (i.e., in the above case, the Ambusher's daddy) from everybody else.

Autre temps, autre moeurs.

This is a book that will stay gentle on your mind, stirring up memories of childhood and family. To have a poet's precision of language and a poet's gift for understanding emotion and a poet's insight into people applied to one of the roughest, toughest, ugliest places in America is an astounding event. And what wealth she finds there; such people, such stories. ∎

HOPE, AGAIN? (1996)

In the wake of the election, The Nation *asked a few contributors for comment. This was Molly Ivins's.*

S o here's Texas, marching militantly in the wrong direction. Another country heard from. We do think you will be amused, however, by our splendid collection of gazoonies in high public office. We are pleased to offer as a member of the House of Representatives our man Ron Paul, who thinks the solution is for us all to become Peruvians. We also bode fair to re-elect Congressman Clueless, Steve Stockman of Beaumont, the Christian Coalition-cum-militia case we sent you two years ago.

As you may have heard, it's not quite over in the Lone Star State. Because thirteen of our thirty Congressional districts were reapportioned at the last minute by a helpful panel of Republican judges, we held open primaries in them on November 5 and will have our runoffs December 10. Such a nice time for a runoff.

Democratic incumbent Ken Bentsen is in a runoff against Dolly Madison McKenna, who is, by our standards, a reasonable Republican. In the 8th District, two Republicans made it to the runoff, Kevin Brady and Gene Fontenot. Gene Fontenot's wife, in a charming pamphlet given to visitors at their palatial mansion, describes how she sought God's counsel on the interior decoration.

The Texas House remains Democratic, but the Senate is still up for grabs: A 15-to-14 Republican edge could be reversed by a special election and a runoff in Lubbock. "Runoff in Lubbock" is a chilling phrase for those who follow Texas politics. We are also pleased to announce the re-election of Senator Drew Nixon of Carthage: Nixon is the fellow who was found by Dallas police in a car with not one but three prostitutes. He explained he thought they were asking for directions.

The case of Ron Paul requires some explanation too. He served in Congress as a Republican from 1976 to 1984 then ran for President as a Libertarian. He resurfaced last year in a primary against Congressman Greg Laughlin, who had switched from D to R. Unhappy Ds may have had something to do with Laughlin's primary defeat, since we have no party-purity law here. The Ds meanwhile nominated an Austin lawyer named Lefty Morris, who campaigned on the slogan "Lefty Is Right!" Ron Paul, in the charming way of Libertarians, is so far right he's sometimes left, which led to general confusion. His earlier call for the repeal of all drug laws and Social Security made little impression on voters, who by the end of the campaign were tired of hearing that the man eats live babies for breakfast. During his retirement, Ron Paul has been putting out a newsletter for fellow Libertarians. In one issue about how to get your money out of the country, he noted that one can purchase citizenship in Peru for a very reasonable $25,000. A good buy, but you'd better act fast: The Peruvians have yet to meet Ron Paul.

My favorite TV ad this year accused an innocuous Democrat

in East Texas of "favoring communism over democracy." This shocking news caused the towers of the Kremlin, in the background, to sway in horror. He won anyway. The Christian Coalition claims to have distributed 7 million pamphlets here this year, including a nauseating number on late-term abortions.

The state, like the aforementioned towers of the Kremlin, was actually swaying toward Democrats a week before Election Day. But then Bill Clinton's Indonesian connection surfaced (has that man ever gotten through a campaign without some scandal breaking?) and Texans started flaking off. Texans don't much like furriners. As our former Governor Bill Clements said during an etiquette lesson preceding the visit of Deng Xiaoping of China to Houston, "Now we have to be nice to this little fella and remember we all like chop suey."

In theory, Texas Democrats are coming up in the world: We have a new party chairman who has introduced the novel concept of using computerized voter lists instead of the old index-cards-in-the-shoebox plan. In the face of the results, we have to say the Ds have hardly managed to stop the hemorrhaging. We had the lowest voter turnout in seventy-two years. The Ds lost all statewide races on the ballot: We elected judges to both the Supreme Court and the Court of Criminal Appeals. We also elected some railroad commissioners, who more or less—mostly less—regulate the oil bidness, and that makes as much sense as anything else in the Great State. ∎

LONE STAR
REPUBLIC (1997)

C alled upon once more in my capacity as the World's Leading Authority on blue-bellied, wall-eyed, lithium-deprived Texas lunatics, I step modestly but confidently into the breach. Yes, friends, I can explain why almost a dozen mush-brained lintheads holed up in the Davis Mountains demanding that Texas become a free country once again. I cannot explain why the national media chose to describe these oxygen-deprived citizens as "Texas separatists"—as though being a Texas separatist were something within the realm of loosely circumscribed sanity—but then, not even Slats Grobnik could explain everything.

The self-proclaimed "Republic of Texas" is a set of folks descended from the Texas property rights movement. The property rights movement, known further west as the Wise Use movement, surfaced here in the summer of 1994, born in a state of high indignation and profound misunderstanding.

The folks in property rights were upset over the prospect that the gummint might take their property without giving them any recompense. These folks were not reassured by the very words in the Constitution that say the gummint cannot take your property without giving you fair value for it. During one memorable exchange on this point, Marshall Kuykendall, president of the group Take Back Texas, replied to some legalistic quibbler who asked for a specific case of gummint taking property. "When Lincoln freed the slaves, he did not pay for them."

You have to admit, ol' Marshall has you there.

Now, while that story is quite true, in fairness, it makes the property rights folks look a lot dumber than they actually are. It is widely understood and accepted, even in Texas, that you cannot do whateverthehell you damn please with your own property if it will have a seriously adverse effect on your neighbors. You cannot be building some plant with a lot of toxic emissions if it will cause the neighbors to die, for example. Reasonable people can agree on that.

But in central Texas, the slightly more communistic area of the state, environmentalists have successfully filed a bunch of lawsuits, leaving the courts pondering how much property has to be set aside to maintain a habitat for two endangered species: the black-capped vireo, a pretty songbird, and the Barton Creek salamander, a critter only a herpetologist could love.

Envision this from the property owner's point of view: Here you are settin' on several acres of increasingly valuable land on the edge of these boomin' cities—either Austin or San Antone. You got these high-tech companies—I.B.M., Texas Instruments, whoever— just beggin' you to let 'em build a nice, new plant on your place. And some fool is goin' to screw this up over a salamander? And while this salamander deal is bein' decided, is anybody goin' to pay you for the money you're losin'?

So there you have the nub of your property rights movement, which also involves more generalized anti-environmentalist sentiment, plus a lot of Fed-cussing.

So how'd we get from fair questions to *las cucarachas* in the Davis Mountains? Easy. The property rights movement always did shade gradually from folks who sound just like every grump you've ever heard grousin' about the goddamn gummint to total fruitcakes. The fruitcake end of the spectrum naturally shaded into the militia movement. As Jim Hamblin of San Marcos, a member of the Texas Constitutional Militia, once inquired reasonably, "Why are they so afraid of a few hundred thousand people with assault rifles?"

But out there on the far end of the militia movement—mostly a bunch of guys who like to play soldier—you find your folks into *The Turner Diaries*, race war and bombing federal buildings. Slippery slopes.

The Republic of Texas in turn has two branches: the nearly normal lunatics who claim to be the official Republic of Texas and the Richard Lance McLaren branch. McLaren has been filing phony liens since 1985 and is splendidly obsessive: He has written thousands and thousands of pages of legal documents, briefs, appeals, warrants, liens, proclamations—a sort of vast parody of the law.

Two things worth noting about the ROT folks. One is, you listen to these guys long enough and they will start to remind you of the kids who used to get so heavily involved in the game Dungeons and Dragons that they lost track of reality. At some point, imagination becomes delusion. And this group delusion is spread through the Internet.

One cannot blame computers for this, since history is full of examples of not just *the folie a deux* but *the folie a large numbers*. But computers do facilitate the phenomenon.

The second important point about ROT and its followers is that they should not be dismissed with the old put-down "Get a life." That's the problem. They can't. Most of them don't have the education or the skills to get and keep a decent job. They're going to spend the rest of their lives in trailer parks. Basically, these guys are Bubba. A little stranger than Bubba usually is, but still Bubba. Maybe a high school education. Twenty, make that almost thirty, years of falling wages. No way to get ahead. And all day they listen to the establishment media tell them the economy is booming. Everyone else is getting rich. Mansions are selling like hotcakes. Big cigars and thick steaks are fashionable again. The angst of the soccer mom is the highest concern of our politicians.

There is so much anger out here. It is taking so many bizarre forms. And most of the media can't even see it: Economic apartheid keeps the bottom half of this society well hidden from the top half. Texas Attorney General Dan Morales says ROT is "terrorism, pure and simple."

We all feel real bad about the one fella who was killed in the deal: We thought we'd gotten out of it without bloodshed, but two of 'em took to the hills. The official explanation is that Mike Matson, 48, was shot by a Texas Department of Criminal Justice dog handler after he had fired on a state helicopter. But it should be noted that Matson had shot three dogs at that point.

Dingbattery, pure and simple I could buy. Terrorism? Because a lot of Americans cannot forgive what happened at Waco and Ruby Ridge? Why should they? Ever heard anyone apologize for those murders? A lot of Americans have no hope, get no help and see their own government as an oppressive force. For them, it is, isn't it? Working-class people are getting screwed by their own government. Its latest start is to cut the capital gains tax and the estate tax that kicks in after a person leaves more than $600,000. More tax breaks for the rich mean a larger share of the tax burden for everybody else.

What we have here is just a little case of misdirected anger. O.K., the U.N. and black helicopters are not the problem. But don't underestimate the anger itself. ∎

SHRUBWATCH (2000)

Every now and again Shrub W. Bush will stop you faster than pullin' on the whoa reins. You can go along for long periods thinkin' to yourself, "Don't agree with him about dog, but he seems like an amiable fellow." And then he says something that sort of makes your teeth hurt. One time W. got to describin' the first time he ran for office—the Boy Bush was an unsuccessful candidate for Congress in 1978 out in West Texas— George Mahon's old seat, district runs from Lubbock to Midland /Odessa to hell and gone. Dubya allowed the race had startled his friends: "They were a little confused about why I was doing this, but at that time, Jimmy Carter was President, and he was trying to control natural gas prices, and I felt the United States was headed toward European-style socialism."

So there you are, trying to envision the very Baptist Brother Carter as a "European-style socialist." Well, Carter does build homes for poor folk without charging, and if that doesn't prove it, what would? Besides, West Texas oilmen, of whom W. was one at the time, think everyone to the left of Trent Lott is a socialist. Reminds me of a story. One time in those very same years the ineffable Good Time Charlie Wilson and Bob Krueger, a Shakespeare scholar last seen in a political ad imitating Arnold Schwarzenegger—two of the finest minds the Peculiar State has ever sent to Congress—cooked up a scheme to deregulate the price of natural gas in such a way that everybody in West Texas would get stinking rich and all you Yankees would have to pay through the nose. They were delicately tap-dancing this masterpiece of reverse socialism through the Commerce Committee one afternoon by the time-tested ploy of sending everyone to sleep (the ploy works best right after lunch) with excruciatingly boring testimony. Wilson swears every Yankee on the committee was snoring when, to his horror, the late Jim Collins, a Dallas Republican, came to and caught the fatal words "gas prices."

"Gas prices?! Gas prices?!" shrieked Collins, waking up all the napping Yankees. "We wouldn't have gas prices this high if it weren't for all this school busing. It's school busing, busing all these Nigras and all these little white children for integration, that's what's driving up gas prices!" And he was off on an anti-busing rant that would not quit. By this time, both Wilson and Krueger were on their hands and knees under the table trying to unplug Collins's mike, but it was too late. The Yankees promptly voted to squelch deregulation of natural gas under the impression that they were carrying on the legacy of Martin Luther King Jr.

Collins is the man who once moved me, in the days when I wrote for the *Dallas Times Herald*, to observe, "If his IQ slips any lower, we'll have to water him twice a day."

Probably the best known of the "whoa" moments with W. Bush comes from an interview with Tucker Carlson printed in *Talk* magazine, concerning the execution of Karla Faye Tucker. Bush has now signed more than 100 warrants of execution, but, as you may recall, the born-again Tucker drew attention both for being female and for having an extensive prison ministry.

In the weeks before the execution, Bush says, Bianca Jagger and a number of other protesters came to Austin to demand clemency for Tucker. "Did you meet with any of them?" I ask. Bush whips around and stares at me. "No, I didn't meet with any of them," he snaps, as though I've just asked the dumbest, most offensive question ever posed. "I didn't meet with Larry King either when he came down for it. I watched his interview with Karla Faye, though. He asked her real difficult questions like, 'What would you say to Governor Bush?'"

"What was her answer?" I wonder.

"Please," Bush whimpers, his lips pursed in mock desperation, "don't kill me."

I must have look shocked—ridiculing the pleas of a condemned prisoner who has since been executed seems odd and cruel, even for someone as militantly anticrime as Bush—because he immediately stops smirking.

Carlson also reported that the exchange mimicked by Bush never took place; Bush made it up.

Well, that was a moment.

Another came during one of Bush's rare appearances on a Sunday chat show. (Ann Richards used to call him "the phantom candidate"; political reporters on his national campaign say he is "in the bubble," rarely let out for an unscripted performance.) Tim Russert asked Bush who on the Supreme Court he most admired. "Scalia," said Bush promptly. And after a second's thought, "and Clarence Thomas."

He sure can pick 'em. If you are a heavy-duty right-winger, as opposed to the moderate, compassionate conservative, Scalia is a good pick. First-rate mind, hideous politics. But no one covering the Court, regardless of politics, has ever chosen Clarence Thomas as a standout. The best I've ever seen written about him, by people who consider Scalia a great Justice, is that he's adequate. Everyone else, including those of no noticeable ideological persuasion, considers "adequate" far too kind.

Thomas, of course, was W.'s daddy's pick. I don't do Siggie Freud myself, being completely unqualified. I leave that to such great minds as Gail Sheehy. But W. does have a daddy problem. Pretty much the entire record of his life is daddy, but it's not his fault. His name is not George W. Smith: What the hell was he supposed to do? Be a big enough fool to throw it all away? Nevertheless, it does sometimes trap him into ridiculous positions.

Twice in the past few weeks we've seen Bush, as we so rarely do, outside the bubble in "debate" with fellow Republican candidates. Myself, I think mah fellow pundits have been entirely too polite. In the first Republican debate in New Hampshire, Bush was, at best, "adequate." In the Arizona debate, he was just bloody awful. Call a spade a spade, troops. If you will pardon a personal note here, I was in hospital, facing a delayed surgical proceeding, during the entire hour-and-a-half debate, and by the end of it, I was screaming, "Put me under the knife! I can't take any more!"

I am a Texan, and we are notoriously soft on our own: I drew the line at Phil Gramm (who wouldn't?), but I can still give a lecture on the virtues of John Connally (when he was a Democrat) on occasion. Texas liberals (screw you, it's not an oxymoron) are persons of large political tolerance. I may intervene from time to time to explain certain political/cultural phenomena—such as why W. Bush keeps leaning into people and touching them—but I plan to limit myself mostly to the geopolitical terrain with which I am most familiar. I know what kind of governor this guy has been—if you expect him to do for the nation what he has for Texas, we need to talk. ■

SHRUB FLUBS
HIS DUB (2001)

h, sure, blame it on Texas. It's all our fault Jim Jeffords walked.[1] Many, many people in Washington are assuming "the Texans" in the White House are responsible for this massive screw-up. Whereas *everybody* in political Austin assumes it. It's often hard to discern the difference between Texas Tough and Texas Stupid.

Sheesh, you play a little hardball, and the guy quits the party over it? So there was a slight miscalculation. As Lyndon Johnson used to say, in his charming fashion, "You got their peckers in your pocket, their hearts and minds will follow." There was just a tiny error about the localization of Jeffords's pecker. Texans are also proud that Senator Phil Gramm, so noted for his charm, also played a role in Jeffords's departure.

Karl Rove, the man known as "Bush's Brain," would never do

---

1 Jeffords, Senator from Vermont, left the Republican Party in 2001 and became an independent. He caucused with the Dems.

anything mean, dirty, petty or tacky. I say this because one of the things I have learned from Rove and Karen Hughes—counselor to His Bushness and also known as Nurse Ratchet—is that if you say something often enough, like "compassionate conservative" or "leave no child behind," the reality makes no difference; people remember only the slogan. (One of the funnier slogans, from Bush's last run for governor, was "end social promotion." Social promotion is the story of Bush's life. The Lege just ended ending social promotion— it doesn't work.) Rove is the master of bait-and-switch politics: Talk moderate, govern right. It took a real moderate like Jeffords to bring this to the media's attention.

One of the post-switch defenses put out by the White House is that Jeffords left the party over a petty social slight: If it was petty of Jeffords to mind not being invited to the ceremony honoring the Teacher of the Year, how petty was it of the Bushes not to invite him? This kind of circular thinking leads people to conclude the Bushies think their own shit don't stink.

When Texas sent the nation Billy Bob Forehead for President, we did, in fact, try to warn y'all about Rove. He not only goes after Democrats, his record of attacking Republicans who cross him is equally distinguished. Rumor and slur campaigns are among his favorite methods. He started using dirty tricks when he was with the College Republicans and has since been linked to the rumors that Ann Richards is a lesbian (a perennial for any woman in politics), that John McCain is crazy as a result of his years in prison camp and several other notable doozies. The campaign against McCain in South Carolina during the primaries was a Rove classic. McCain was simultaneously rumored to be gay and a tomcat who cheats on his wife, who in turn was rumored to be a drug addict. The news that

McCain has a black daughter (adopted from Bangladesh) was spread judiciously under the radar of the national media. Anonymous leaflets put under the windshield wipers of cars parked at white fundamentalist churches on Sunday are good for this purpose, as are certain radio call-in shows.

According to the May 14 issue of the conservative *Weekly Standard*, before Jeffords switched: "The White House and Senate sources say it [the social snub] was a taste of things to come for Jeffords. 'The White House is not giving specifics,' says a senior GOP source. 'But there's a one- or two-year plan to punish him for his behavior. And it's stuff that may hurt him, but stuff that's not going to draw a significant amount of attention. So they're going to get him.'" This fits so well with Rove's past patterns that the reaction to Jeffords's switch at the Texas capitol was unanimous—a Rove play that went bad.

In intraparty fights, Rove often uses money. Tom Pauken is a Dallas lawyer and sort of a right-wing populist who was elected chairman of the state party against Rove's wishes: He was the candidate of the Christian right, and the Bushies favored a more establishment candidate. So after Pauken won, Rove called the big party donors, and their money suddenly went to political accounts controlled by Rove rather than to the state party. Then two sort of wacko Christian Republicans on the state school board went to New Hampshire last year to endorse Steve Forbes and returned to find their opponents flush with money from Bush givers: a rare confluence of Rove's revenge and general civic betterment. "You don't cross Karl Rove and not expect repercussions," said Bob Offutt of the state school board after he lost the primary.

Meanwhile, the Texas capitol has just lived through a session-long hangover from the Bush years. Tax cuts in two successive sessions, '97 and '99, left the state's cupboard bare. There was no money for getting up to average in anything: Our state motto is still "Forever 48th." Despite a record $114 billion budget (that's for two years), we are not even sure many of our miserly programs will keep pace with population growth. If they didn't cost money, a lot of things Bush opposed could get done this session. The Lege passed a hate crimes bill, gave prison inmates in the Cowboy Gulag access to DNA testing and made it illegal to put kids in the back of your pickup. Unfortunately, they could not bring themselves to stop executing the retarded. We did finally get health insurance for teachers—now there's a coup. Despite a rousing economy, all the money was blown by Bush in tax cuts that came to a Big Mac a month. Most Texans never saw even that much, since the desperate school districts hiked their tax rates as soon as the state cut its.

The lobbyists, who know more than anyone else, are betting Texas will have to go to an income tax within two sessions because of the Bush cuts. A state income tax is anathema here, and has been desperately avoided by generations of pols.

Bush was replaced by his exceedingly Lite Guv Rick Perry, who has really good hair. Governor Goodhair is not the sharpest knife in the drawer. But the chair of a major House committee says, "Goodhair is much more engaged as governor than Bush was." As the refrain of the country song goes, "O Please, Dear God, Not Another One." ∎

FLIGHT OF THE KILLER D'S (2003)

They're back now, but Texas' few living elected Democrats, who fled to Oklahoma pursued by minions of the law, are said to remain unrepentant. The proximate cause was a redistricting map, but the real reason was a session-long display of meanness and unfairness that finally became unbearable. Faced with a $10 billion deficit, the Republicans decided to outlaw gay marriage. Then they kicked 250,000 poor children off a health insurance program that is mostly paid for by the Feds. And when the handicapped came to the capital to protest cuts in their services, the governor had them arrested.

These are Shiite Republicans—they don't compromise, they don't deal, they don't look for the middle way. Because they believe they're right. They think it's them against evil. And everybody who ain't them is evil. I'm just warning you: This is about to happen everywhere. The whole country is being turned into the state whose proudest boast is that sometimes we're ahead of Mississippi.

After the Democrats' Big Bolt, the Republicans were left without a quorum. Bills died by the dozen as the lawmakers wanted by the law bollixed up the legislative works (bills not through second reading as of May 15 die automatically, a bit of legislative process the fleeing Dems cunningly used to their advantage). Governor Goodhair Perry, who keeps saying he wants more civility and bipartisanship, denounced the AWOL solons as "cowardly" and "childish." He asked neighboring governors to arrest the perps on sight, leading New Mexico Attorney General Patricia Madrid to put out an all-points bulletin on any politicians "in favor of health care for the needy and against tax cuts for the wealthy." Speaker Tom Craddick, the tyrant whose insupportable conduct forced these brave Democratic heroes to leave their native heath, said he refused to negotiate and that the Killer D's were embarrassing the State of Texas.

But the real embarrassment was US House majority leader Tom "The Hammer" DeLay, who admitted that the Republicans had sought the assistance of the federales in going after the recalcitrant D's. That, apparently, is how the Homeland Security Department, which is supposed to be making America safe from foreign terrorists, ended up tracking a plane belonging to one of the Democrats fighting against the redistricting bill to Ardmore, Oklahoma. This isn't just weird Texas politics—creepin' fascism, that's what we're looking at.

The redistricting map that touched off this mess is a masterpiece, a veritable Dadaist work reminiscent of Salvador Dali's more lunatic productions. But the Democrats' action has nothing to do with "payback." The Texas Congressional redistricting plan currently in effect was drawn by the courts and was a great disappointment to the Democrats.

Nor is Speaker Craddick's session-long performance combining the best elements of Dracula and The Eggplant That Ate Chicago payback for some heavy-handed Democratic domination. For the past ten years, the Speaker of the House has been a decent and exceptionally fair man named Pete Laney. If you don't believe me, go ask George W. Bush.

The Democrats came home heroes to their people. A Democrat from Boise, Idaho, said he planned to confront the state's legislative D's with headlines and pictures of the Texas Killer D's and to label the montage "Democrats With Cojones." Unfortunately, it was pointed out, there aren't enough Idaho Democrats to break a quorum. ∎

IS TEXAS AMERICA? (2003)

This piece was written for a collection *In These United States*, edited by John Leonard (Nation Books).

Well, sheesh. I don't know whether to warn you that because George Dubya Bush is President the whole damn country is about to be turned into Texas (a singularly horrible fate: as the country song has it: "Lubbock on Everythang") or if I should try to stand up for us and convince the rest of the country we're not all that insane.

Truth is, I've spent much of my life trying, unsuccessfully, to explode the myths about Texas. One attempts to explain—with all good will, historical evidence, nasty statistics and just a bow of recognition to our racism—that Texas is not *The Alamo* starring John Wayne. We're not *Giant*, we ain't a John Ford western. The first real Texan I ever saw on TV was *King of the Hill*'s Boomhauer, the guy who's always drinking beer and you can't understand a word he says.

So, how come trying to explode myths about Texas always winds up reinforcing them? After all these years, I do not think it is my fault. The fact is, it's a damned peculiar place. Given all the horseshit, there's bound to be a pony in here somewhere. Just by trying to be honest about it, one accidentally underlines its sheer strangeness.

Here's the deal on Texas. It's big. So big there's about five distinct and different places here, separated from one another geologically, topographically, botanically, ethnically, culturally and climatically. Hence our boring habit of specifying East, West and South Texas, plus the Panhandle and the Hill Country. The majority of the state's blacks live in East Texas, making it more like the Old South than the Old South is anymore. West Texas is, more or less, like *Giant*, except, like every place else in the state, it has an incurable tendency toward the tacky and all the cowboys are brown. South Texas is 80 percent Hispanic and a weird amalgam of cultures. You get names now like Shannon Rodriguez, Hannah Gonzalez and Tiffany Ruiz. Even the Anglos speak English with a Spanish accent. The Panhandle, which sticks up to damn near Kansas, is High Plains, like one of those square states, Nebraska or the Dakotas, except more brown folks. The Hill Country, smack dab in the middle, resembles nothing else in the state.

Plus, plopped on top of all this, we have three huge cities, all among the ten largest in the country. Houston is Los Angeles with the climate of Calcutta, Dallas is Dutch (clean, orderly and conformist), while San Antonio is Monterrey North. Many years ago I wrote of this state: "The reason the sky is bigger here is because there aren't any trees. The reason folks here eat grits is because they ain't got no taste. Cowboys mostly stink and it's hot, oh God, is it hot…. Texas is a mosaic of cultures, which overlap in several parts of the state, with the darker layers on the bottom. The cultures are black, Chicano, Southern, freak, suburban and shitkicker. (Shitkicker is dominant.) They are all rotten for women." All that's changed in thirty years is that suburban is now dominant, shitkicker isn't so ugly as it once was and the freaks are now Goths or something. So it could be argued we're becoming more civilized.

In fact, it was always easy to argue that: Texas has symphony orchestras and great universities and perfect jewels of art museums (mostly in Fort Worth, of all places). It has lots of people who birdwatch, write PhD theses on esoteric subjects and speak French, for chrissake. But what still makes Texas Texas is that it's ignorant, cantankerous and ridiculously friendly. Texas is still resistant to Howard Johnsons, Interstate highways and some forms of phoniness. It is the place least likely to become a replica of everyplace else. It's authentically awful, comic and weirdly charming, all at the same time.

Culturally, Texans rather resemble both Alaskans (hunt, fish, hate government) and Australians (drink beer, hate snobs). The food is quite good—Mexican, barbecue, chili, shrimp and chicken-fried steak, an acquired taste. The music is country, blues, folk, mariachi, rockabilly and everything else you can think of. Mexican music—*norteño*, *ranchero*—-is poised to cross over, as black music did in the 1950s.

If you want to understand George W. Bush—unlike his daddy, an unfortunate example of a truly Texas-identified citizen—you have to stretch your imagination around a weird Texas amalgam: religion, anti-intellectualism and machismo. All big, deep strains here, but still an odd combination. Then add that Bush is just another li'l upper-class white boy out trying to prove he's tough.

The politics are probably the weirdest thing about Texas. The state has gone from one-party Democrat to one-party Republican in thirty years. Lyndon said when he signed the Civil Rights Act in 1964 that it would take two generations and cost the Democrats the South. Right on both counts. We like to think we're "past race" in Texas, but of course East Texas remains an ugly, glaring exception. After James Byrd Jr. was dragged to death near Jasper, only one prominent white politician attended his funeral—US Senator Kay Bailey Hutchison. Dubya, then governor, put the kibosh on the anti-hate crimes bill named in Byrd's memory. (The deal-breaker for Bush was including gays and lesbians. At a meeting last year of the Texas Civil Liberties Union board, vicious hate crimes against gays in both Dallas and Houston were discussed. I asked the board member from Midland if they'd been having any trouble with gay-bashing out there. "Hell, honey," she said, with that disastrous frankness one can grow so fond of, "there's not a gay in Midland would come out of the closet for fear people would think they're a Democrat.")

Among the various strains of Texas right wingism (it is factually incorrect to call it conservatism) is some leftover loony John Birchism, now morphed into militias; country-club economic conservatism, à la George Bush *père*; and the usual batty anti-government strain. Of course Texas grew on the tender mercies of the federal government—rural electrification, dams, generations of master pork-barrel politicians and vast subsidies to the oil and gas industry. But that has never interfered with Texans' touching but entirely erroneous belief that this is the Frontier, and that in the Old West every man pulled his own weight and depended on no one else. The myth of rugged individualism continues to afflict a generation raised entirely in suburbs with names like Flowering Forest Hills of Lubbock.

The Populist movement was born in the Texas Hill Country,

as genuinely democratic an uprising as this country has ever known. It produced legendary politicians for generations, including Ralph Yarborough, Sam Rayburn, Lyndon and even into the 1990s, with Agriculture Commissioner Jim Hightower. I think it is not gone, but only sleeping.

Texans retain an exaggerated sense of state identification, routinely identifying themselves when abroad as Texans, rather than Americans or from the United States. That aggravated provincialism has three sources. First, the state is so big (though not so big as Alaska, as they are sure to remind us) that it can take a couple of days hard travel just to get out of it. Second, we reinforce the sense of difference by requiring kids to study Texas history, including roughly ten years as an independent country. In state colleges, the course in Texas government is mandatory. Third, even national advertising campaigns pitch brands with a Texas accent here and certain products, like the pickup truck, are almost invariably sold with a Texas pitch. (Makes sense: Texas leads the nation with more than four million registered pickups.)

The founding myth is the Alamo. I was raised on the Revised Standard Version, which holds that while it was stupid of Travis and the gang to be there at all (Sam Houston told them to get the hell out), it was still an amazing last stand. Stephen Harrigan in *The Gates of the Alamo* is closer to reality, but even he admits in the end there was something romantic and even noble about the episode, like having served in the Abraham Lincoln Brigade during the Spanish Civil War.

According to the demographers at Texas A&M (itself a source of much Texas lore), Texas will become "majority minority" in 2008. Unfortunately, we won't see it in the voting patterns for at least a generation, and by then the Republicans will have the state so tied up by redistricting (recently the subject of a massive standoff, now over, in the legislature), it's unlikely to shift for another generation beyond that. The Christian right is heavily dominant in the Texas Republican Party. It was the genius of Karl Rove/George W. Bush to straddle the divide between the Christian right and the country club conservatives, which is actually a significant class split. The politics of resentment plays a large role on the Christian right: Fundamentalists are perfectly aware that they are held in contempt by "the intellectuals." (William Brann of Waco once observed, "The trouble with our Texas Baptists is that we do not hold them under water long enough." He was shot to death by an irate Baptist.) In Texas, "intellectual" is often used as a synonym for "snob." George W. Bush perfectly exemplifies that attitude.

Here in the National Laboratory for Bad Government, we have an antiquated and regressive tax structure—high property, high sales, no income tax. We consistently rank near the bottom by every measure of social service, education and quality of life (leading to one of our state mottoes, "Thank God for Mississippi"). Yet the state is incredibly rich in more than natural resources. The economy is now fully diversified, so plunges in the oil market can no longer throw the state into the bust cycle.

It is widely believed in Texas that the highest purpose of government is to create "a healthy bidness climate." The legislature is so dominated by special interests that the gallery where the lobbyists sit is called "the owners' box." The consequences of unregulated capitalism, of special interests being able to buy government through campaign contributions, are more evident here because Texas is "first and worst" in this area. That Enron was a Texas company is no accident: Texas was also Ground Zero in the savings-and-loan scandals, is continually the site of major ripoffs by the insurance industry and has a rich history of gigantic chicanery going way back. Leland Beatty, an agricultural consultant, calls Enron "Billie Sol Estes Goes to College." Economists call it "control fraud" when a corporation is rotten from the head down. I sometimes think Texas government is a case of control fraud too.

We are currently saddled with a right-wing ideologue sugar daddy, James Leininger out of San Antonio, who gives immense campaign contributions and wants school vouchers, abstinence education and the like in return. The result is a crew of breathtakingly right-wing legislators. This session, Representative Debbie Riddle of Houston said during a hearing, "Where did this idea come from that everybody deserves free education, free medical care, free whatever? It comes from Moscow, from Russia. It comes straight out of the pit of hell."

Texans for Lawsuit Reform, a k a the bidness lobby, is a major player and has effectively eviscerated the judiciary with a two-pronged attack. While round after round of "tort reform" was shoved through the legislature, closing off access to the courts and protecting corporations from liability for their misdeeds, Karl Rove was busy electing all nine state Supreme Court justices. So even if you should somehow manage to get into court, you are faced with a bench noted for its canine fidelity to corporate special interests.

Here's how we make progress in Texas. Two summers ago, Governor Goodhair Perry (the man has a head of hair every Texan can be proud of, regardless of party) appointed an Enron executive to the Public Utilities Commission. The next day, Governor Goodhair got a $25,000 check from Ken Lay. Some thought there might be a connection. The guv was forced to hold a press conference, at which he explained that the whole thing was "totally coincidental." So that was a big relief.

We don't have a sunshine law in Texas; it's more like a partly cloudy law. But even here a major state appointee has to fill out a bunch of forms that are then public record. When the governor's office put out the forms on the Enron guy, members of the press, that alert guardian watchdog of democracy, noticed that the question about any unfortunate involvement with law enforcement looked funny. The governor's office had whited out the answers. A sophisticated cover-up. The alert guardian watchdogs were on the trail. We soon uncovered a couple of minor traffic violations and the following item: While out hunting a few years earlier, the Enron guy accidentally shot a whooping crane. As a result he had to pay a $15,000 fine under what is known in Texas as the In Danger Species Act. We print this. A state full of sympathetic hunters reacted with, "Hell, anybody could accidentally shoot a whooper." But the press stayed on the story and was able to report that the guy shot the whooper while on a goose hunt. Now the whooper is a large bird—runs up to five feet tall. The goose—short. Now we have a state full of hunters saying, "Hell, if this boy is too dumb to tell a whooper from a goose, maybe he shouldn't be regulatin' public utilities." He was forced to resign.

As Willie Nelson sings, if we couldn't laugh, we would all go insane. This is our redeeming social value and perhaps our one gift to progressives outside our borders. We do laugh. We have no choice. We have to have fun while trying to stave off the forces of darkness because we hardly ever win, so it's the only fun we get to have. We find beer and imagination helpful. The Billion Bubba March, the Spam-o-rama, the time we mooned the Klan, being embedded with the troops at the Holiday Inn in Ardmore, Oklahoma, singing

"I'm Just an Asshole from E1 Paso" with Kinky Friedman and the Texas Jewboys, and "Up Against the Wall, Redneck Mother" with Ray Wylie Hubbard laughing at the loonies in the Lege—does it get better than this? The late Bill Kugle of Athens is buried in the Texas State Cemetery. On the front of his stone are listed his service in the Marines in World War II, his years in the legislature, other titles and honors. On the back of the stone is, "He never voted for a Republican and never had much to do with them either."

We have lost some great freedom fighters in Texas during the past year. Billie Cart, the great Houston political organizer (you'd've loved her: She got invited to the White House during the middle of the Monica mess, sashayed through the receiving line, looked Bill Clinton in the eye and said, "You dumb son of a bitch"), always said she wanted her funeral to be like her whole life in politics: It should start half an hour late, she wanted a balanced delegation of pallbearers—one black, one brown, two women—and she wanted an open casket and a name tag stuck over her left tit that said, "Hi there! My name is Billie Carr." We did it all for her.

At the funeral of Malcolm McGregor, the beloved legislator and bibliophile from E1 Paso, we heard "The Eyes of Texas" and the Aggie War Hymn played on the bagpipes. At the service for Maury Maverick Jr. of San Antonio, and at his request, J. Frank Dobie's poem "The Mustangs" was read by the poet Naomi Shihab Nye. The last stanza is:

> So sometimes yet, in the realities of silence and solitude,
> For a few people unhampered a while by things,
> The mustangs walk out with dawn, stand high, then
> Sweep away, wild with sheer life, and free, free, free—
> Free of all confines of time and flesh.   ■

JACK GORDON:
OBITUARY (2006)

Jack Gordon, known as "the unabashedly liberal conscience of Florida's State Senate," was a unique combination of scholar, wit and idealist as well as a remarkably effective practical politician. His stands should have made him anathema to the Florida legislature of the 1970s and '80s, still dominated by good ol' boys: Gordon opposed the death penalty, favored the Equal Rights Amendment and legalizing marijuana, and was a longtime champion of civil rights and school integration.

Instead, Gordon was chosen majority leader by his colleagues, who respected his fairness, his civility and his legislative wiliness. That he also happened to be a successful banker gave him street cred with conservatives. Gordon was rather fond of many of the more colorful specimens of good ol' boy with whom he served, and he was skillful at finding common ground with them. He was a natural teacher and believed part of his job was to use debate to elucidate issues, to encourage problem-solving. As a result, his rich legacy includes one of the most advanced amendments on privacy rights in any state Constitution as well as Florida's homestead property-tax exemption. He outlawed discrimination at country clubs and championed education. "The Gordon Rule," which requires more math and writing courses, raises the skill level of Florida college students. He was the kind of legislator who devoted time to thankless tasks like reorganizing the Department of Health and Rehabilitative Services and creating the Department of Corrections, grunt work that makes an enormous difference in the lives of people with no power.

Gordon's politics were always progressive, and he fondly recalled the furious debates at the Miami Beach chess club, where old Bolsheviks and old Mensheviks still went after each other. He was a friend and business partner of the great Florida populist Claude Pepper; after Pepper's death Gordon briefly considered a run for his Congressional seat. Although he was a brilliant politician, he was constitutionally incapable of dishonesty. The campaign consultants decided he would make a terrible candidate.

Gordon retired from the State Senate in 1992, observing that the money in politics had become overwhelming. He founded the Hospice Foundation of America and served on Rosalyn Carter's mental health task force. He was a remarkable public servant and also just a lovely man. He is remembered by those who knew him as the most brilliant or the kindest man they ever met. Few things were more fun than seeing Jack Gordon's ascetic face light up and his eyes begin to twinkle as he recognized something funny in whatever was under discussion—then all you had to do was sit back and wait for the quiet wisecrack. ∎